CLASS

CLASS

NOTES ON DANCE CLASSES AROUND THE WORLD
1915-1980

RUTH PAGE

Edited and Additional Notes
ANDREW M. WENTINK
Drawings
ANDRÉ DELFAU

PRINCETON BOOK COMPANY, PUBLISHERS, PRINCETON, NEW JERSEY

To
LARRY LONG
With Love

CONTENTS

ACKNOWLEDGMENTS

My most heartfelt thanks, as always, to André Delfau for his original and evocative illustrations of modern and ethnic dance; many thanks to Frank Derbas, for his photo reproduction of the historical photographs from the personal collection of Ruth Page and from the Ruth Page Collection in the Dance Collection, Performing Arts Research Center, The New York Public Library at Lincoln Center, and to Genevieve Oswald, Curator of the Dance Collection, and her staff. My appreciation and thanks to Barbara Palfy, for her diligent and painstaking copyediting of this complicated manuscript; and special thanks and gratitude to Charles H. Woodford, for his interest in publishing *Class* and for his belief in and enthusiasm for the project from the outset.

Ruth Page
Chicago, 1983

PREFACE

This book is a record of an education in dance—an eclectic education, to be sure, but in America in the first decades of this century, little else was possible. Well-rounded dance training was hard to come by. Those who found in themselves a burning desire to dance chose either to be self-taught after a few basic classes (modern dance pioneers Loie Fuller, Isadora Duncan, and Ruth St. Denis did so) or to look anywhere and everywhere for teachers who would impart something as yet unknown, something to help develop unfulfilled potential in the eager dancer.

Ruth Page was a dancer of the second category, but a choreographer of the first. She refused to conform to one style. Her dances and ballets were created individually, dictated by the inherent logic of her dance conception. At the outset, Page, at age fifteen, realized that she must study with teachers of all kinds of dancing, whenever and wherever she could. Also, from the beginning, she took copious notes on classes to remind her of steps of particular interest, difficulty, or inspiration. She continued this practice throughout her life.

This selection is gleaned from more than fifteen manuscript note-books,[1] the earliest dated 1915. Since interest and need determined the taking of these notes, complete classes are rarely recorded. However, the notes do offer glimpses of what ballet, modern, and ethnic classes were like in the first half of the century.[2]

Prior to 1915, few dancing schools of merit existed except in New York City, where many schools taught all types of stage dancing in addition to ballet. Since there were no full-fledged ballet companies, dancers often found work in vaudeville, Broadway musicals and revues, and motion picture prologues. Louis Chalif and Elizavetta Menzeli, with studios located in New York, were dominant forces in American dance education. Chalif, a Russian, and Mme. Menzeli, a pupil of Paul Taglioni, represented the two nations that had attained the highest level of achievement in balletic style and technique. Ruth Page benefited from training with teachers of both nationalities.

Adolph Bolm, a Russian émigré from the Maryinsky Imperial Ballet and Diaghilev's Ballets Russes, was the most influential of Page's early teachers. The notes on his classes reveal that he, like many teachers of the period, who were relocated former dancers of distinction, taught from necessity rather than from inclination. The unconventional combinations and unsystematic approach to teaching are a reflection of a mind more concerned with performing and choreography than with the niceties of classroom technique. Bolm's classes lacked the sophistication

---

[1]Most of these are in the Ruth Page Collection in the Dance Collection, The New York Public Library at Lincoln Center.

[2]Although the attempt was made to include representative photographs for each section, selection ultimately had to be made from what was available.

and strict structure of his own teacher, Enrico Cecchetti, yet the "aber-rations" in his method projected the force of individuality. The invalu-able encouragement of personality in a young dancer is a sadly missing asset in the classes of many teachers today, who concentrate solely on placement and technique.

Italian teachers, such as Luigi Albertieri and Cia Fornaroli, were also protégés of the great Cecchetti, steeped in his style and technique and dedicated to his principles. Yet, even they altered his approach to teach-ing and class sequence to suit their individual temperaments, technical strengths and preferences, and the abilities of their students. Academic strictness aside, these teachers found inspiring the energy of American dancers and encouraged them to seek the limits of their own potential, rather than demanding from them a conformity to a particular method or indulgence in technique alone.

Page's notes on ballet classes are historically valuable as an indication of how teaching methods have evolved from Zalewski and Bolm to Edna McRae and Larry Long. Teachers and students curious enough to investi-gate these notes might find them useful as a starting point for developing original combinations.

It was initially intended to supply missing counts and port de bras. It became evident, however, that it is impossible to know what was done *exactly* in these classes over fifty years ago. Moreover, when professional dancers were asked to execute these combinations, an accompanying port de bras formed instinctively. Therefore, for the sake of historical validity, the notes have been left largely the way they were recorded at the time, but edited for consistency and conformity to standard termi-nology usage, rather than presented in facsimile transcription.

In the German Expressionism of Mary Wigman and Harald Kreutzberg, the approach to movement was so personalized and natural that the notes are left virtually intact, documenting how and what these two dance giants taught. Expressed in terms meaningful to Ruth Page as she observed them, the movements retain their original "feel." The notes on Wigman and Kreutzberg classes were so extensive (over seventy manuscript pages) that a representative selection has been made.

The notes on ethnic dance are the most elusive because the learning of these dances is largely, as Page says, "intuitive." She was fortunate in being encouraged to study elsewhere by Bolm, who not only brought her to Cecchetti, but sent her to the great exponent of Spanish dance, Aurora Arriaza. Her appetite whetted, Page made it a point to study at the source —with Maestro Realito in Seville and with the gypsies at Granada—on various trips to Europe.

In 1928-29, she made a solo tour of the Orient, during which she studied the indigenous dances. Her notations of these dances, especially those of Bali, are a notable achievement. Few Western dancers, other than Anna Pavlova and the Denishawn Company, had ever seen these dances before Ruth Page observed and recorded them. Of course, certain words and phrases used to describe the movements of this highly stylized art (e.g., "shimmy," "wiggle") indicate Page's background as an American. Yet, the fact that Ruth Page learned these dances entirely by observation and imitation, and attempted to approximate their essence in words, is remarkable.

Even today, relatively few dancers learn how to record the art to which they dedicate their lives. Despite the success and wide official use of the Laban, Benesh, and Sutton notation systems, most dancers have little opportunity to study them to a degree of practical proficiency. Thus, if they wish to record classes or choreography, dancers still fall back on personal shorthand systems, not very different from those Ruth Page used sixty-five years ago. We can only be grateful that she felt the need to document moments of classes with teachers around the world who have become legend by laying the foundations of dance training in this century.

Andrew Mark Wentink

ABBREVIATIONS AND OTHER SPECIAL USAGES

ABBREVIATIONS

demi-pte, demi-pointe; *diag,* diagonal (ly); *ft,* foot; *fwd,* forward; *L,* left; *pte,* pointe; *pte-tendue,* pointe tendue; *pos,* position; *R,* right.

SPECIAL USAGES

À la seconde is used when working leg is moving to or held in 2nd pos; 2nd pos is used to describe feet and arms.

Assemblé back is used when working leg moves from 5th pos front to 5th pos back.

Assemblé fwd is used when working leg moves from 5th pos back to 5th pos front.

Assemblé en arrière is used when working leg moves from 5th pos (or open) back to 5th pos back.

Assemblé en avant is used when working leg moves from 5th pos (or open) front to 5th pos front.

In ethnic dance, the words "wiggle" and "jiggle" imply a rapid vibratory movement.

C1, C2, etc. are derived from Cecchetti's *Manual:*

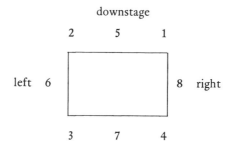

INTRODUCTION

Next to performing, class is the most important thing in a dancer's life. Unlike other artists, dancers usually do not like to practice alone. In my youth, there was no official school in America, as there was in Russia, France, or Italy, where you knew you would get a good training. You had to shop around. As I had a bad memory, I made notes on dance classes of all kinds that I took all over the world. In those days, no one taught dancers how to write down classes or dances, so you had to devise a method of your own. Sometimes, I did not write out a full step, just the parts that interested me particularly. So my notes are often incomplete. I wrote these notes just for myself, and while they may be a little difficult to figure out, they give an idea of and a feeling for the different approaches and personalities of the many teachers with whom I studied.

Ballet is comparatively easy to write out because there is a written vocabulary in French which corresponds to every step, and the style of execution varies only slightly among the major French, Russian, and Italian schools. Even when I was just a beginner, the notes that I put down could be understood, up to a point, by anyone who studied ballet.

When I went to the Orient, however, the problem of writing out ethnic dances was more difficult. The experience was foreign to my eyes and, while there probably was a classic vocabulary for the dances of Japan, China, and the countries of Indochina and Indonesia, I was totally unaware of it. Besides that, the method of teaching was different. There, they taught you actual traditional or classical dances rather than classroom steps, so I described what I saw, only occasionally referring to the ballet steps and positions that they resembled. Of course, it is much simpler to learn by studying films, which I took even then, but one needs, ideally, both the films and the notation.

From my experience with the few modern dancers with whom I studied —chiefly exponents of the so-called German Expressionism—"modern" classes varied tremendously from teacher to teacher. As far as I knew, there were no set classes as there are in ballet, although the Martha Graham School has since developed definitive classes. Each teacher was more individual than in ballet, and sometimes the classes were totally improvised.

To write out a modern class presented many problems. The steps did not have names and, therefore, I could only note what I saw and what I felt. Patterns were sometimes as important as the steps; the contracting and relaxing action in the center of the body was very hard to describe in words. It was the expressivity *required from all parts of the body that made it, in many cases, different and more difficult than simple calisthenic-type exercises, which much of it resembled. You did not always have to point your toes or straighten your knees, which made it more enjoyable as a free and natural way to move. However, although there were no set classes in the traditional sense, there was most definitely an individual technique that characterized the work of each major modern dancer.*

A dancer needs a class on performance nights that differs from one when he is just studying, but in either case, class *is the thing of utmost importance in his life. I love to watch the bodies of the various dancers I meet in class, and I like to see how their bodies are ruled by their minds. The ideal dancer is a combination of brains and brawn that is decidedly fascinating. Dancing is not only hard work, it is also great fun and daily class is an excellent habit to cultivate.*

Ruth Page

Ballet

B A L L E T is the form of theatrical dance studied most widely, I would say. Its classes are most familiar to us all, but they make a fascinating study because of the endless variety of teaching methods. Although the basic correctness of all styles remains the same—a plié can be done in only one way to be correct; positions (e.g., écarté, éffacé, croisé) are always the same—what teachers invent in the way of combinations differs considerably from country to country and from teacher to teacher.

Over the years, ballet classes have changed a great deal. Enrico Cecchetti was once considered the "God of Classical Ballet." Most teachers of the time (until the mid-1930s) followed the basic tenets of his method, no matter how different their individual styles. Today, the Cecchetti method is considered by some to be old-fashioned, too academic and mild. Cecchetti's barre, for example, lasted about twenty minutes and was the same every day. Nowadays, most barres last forty-five minutes, at least. The combinations are very long and complicated in movement and rhythm, and much time is spent on correct body placement. Ironically, many teachers are saying the same things Cecchetti said so long ago, only taking much longer to say it.

The purpose of the barre used to be to warm up the body in preparation for adagio and allegro work in the center. It now seems to have evolved into an end in itself. With nearly half, if not three-quarters, of the class spent at the barre, there is very little time left for adagio, pirouettes, jumps, and more complex combinations in the center.

Classical ballet has become more and more technically demanding. The virtuosity of today's dancers, compared to those in my day, is truly prodigious.

Jan Zalewski

JAN ZALEWSKI B. 1880?

Jan Zalewski, though evident in programs as a dancer in Anna Pavlova's company for many years, seems to elude any firm documentation of his personal background and dance training or his life following his years with Pavlova. Ruth Page's reminiscences and photographs provide more information than any available printed source. For a glimpse of dance training in early twentieth-century America and its origins, one must turn to the pioneers, Louis Chalif and Elizavetta Menzeli.

Louis Chalif (1876–1948) was born in Odessa, Russia. At age nine, he started dance training at the Odessa Municipal Theatre Ballet School, where his teachers were Alfred Bekefi, Ivan Savitsky, and Thomas Nijinsky, father of Vaslav and Bronislava. Graduating in 1893, Chalif became a member of the Odessa ballet company, its ballet master in 1897, and premier danseur in 1903.

In 1904, Chalif came to the United States and performed briefly at the Metropolitan Opera under the direction of Luigi Albertieri. In 1905, Dr. Luther H. Gulick invited Chalif to teach at Teachers College of New York University. This was the beginning of a career that brought him to the forefront of the movement that introduced ballet dancing to the average American child. His introductory classes for the American Society of Professors of Dancing were too difficult for the membership; thereafter, the demand for his training of dance teachers was constant. Among his "innovations" were the reintroduction to ballet classes of *barre* exercises, precise technical terms, and the use of classical music to accompany instruction, rather than the rhythmic pounding of a cane.

The Chalif Russian Normal School of Dancing opened in 1907, and became the "most exclusive school for amateur dancing in New York." Chalif's influence was enormously enhanced by the publication and nationwide distribution of his vast library of dances, class instructions, and notes, to which Ruth Page refers. He arranged over one thousand of these dances, and his system was collected in *Dance: A Basic Educational Technique,* edited by Frederick Rand Rogers and published in 1941.

Elizavetta Menzeli (1850–1934) was as "imposing" as Ruth Page remembers her to be. Not only did Mme. Menzeli direct her school of Ballet, Fancy, Stage and Artistic Dancing, at 22 East 16th Street, which she opened in 1890, but promoted herself as "Originator, Composer, Producer, Director, Instructor, and Coach of Ballets, Pantomimes, Plays, Operettas, Musical Comedies, Kermesses, Gold and Silver Jubilees, Historical Pageants and Festivals for all Occasions, Sketches, Choruses, Song and Dance Steps," and teacher of "Up-to-Date Novelties, Classic, Ballet, Toe, Greek, Fancy, National, Eccentric, Comic, Grotesque" as well as Delsartean gestures. There were also departments of music and speech arts, directed by Mr. B. Russell Throckmorton, who taught a 1910 course in public speaking for women.

Elizavetta Menzeli teaching class, ca. 1910

Mme. Menzeli taught a professional class every morning from ten to half-past eleven. Classes cost $30.00 a month, private lessons (trial, $6; single class, $10; six classes, $30), and scholarships were offered. For those who could not attend the Menzeli school in New York, but wanted training in "Artistic dancing and pantomime in all its branches. Elocution for Pulpit, Stage, Platform and Parlor. Dramatic Art in its full meaning and purpose, and Music thorough in its every form," instructions were mailed upon request (and for a fee).

If all of this seems extraordinary for one person to have offered, it was not unusual at the time: Elizavetta was one of the famous Menzeli sisters who danced at Niblo's Garden in the last quarter of the nineteenth century; was considered, along with Maria Bonfanti, one of the two best dancers on the American stage; and had staged the ballet for the premiere of Verdi's *Aida* in Cairo in 1870, and its American premiere by "the Italian Opera Company" in 1877.

Among the illustrious Menzeli pupils were Ruth St. Denis, Maud Allan, Stefano Mascagno, Gertrude Hoffman, Maude Adams, and Julia Marlowe, all of whom heeded the call:

> *Trust to art, not chance,*
> *for they move easiest who have*
> *learned to dance.*

There is nothing more difficult than finding the right ballet classes on a beginner level, and my beginnings were more unusual than most. My earliest dance training was not classical at all, but "fancy dancing" lessons with Miss Anna Stanton in Indianapolis. I suppose we did not learn too much about discipline in Miss Stanton's classes, but we girls had a lot of fun trying to decipher the "learn to dance by mail" courses of Louis Chalif, whose popular dances were based on amusing subjects that children would find interesting. My first taste of classical ballet came, I think, when my mother took me to New York while I was still in high school. I had one week of classes with the imposing Elizavetta Menzeli at her "Knickerbocker Conservatory, School of Ballet, Fancy, Stage and Society Dancing."

My first exposure to real ballet training on a regular basis came in classes with Jan Zalewski, a member of Anna Pavlova's company. Pavlova sent Zalewski, a Polish dancer, to Indianapolis on his holiday, so that he could give me a lesson every day. Since I was essentially a raw beginner, his lessons were very important to me. He was nice enough, as a person, but rather uninspiring to a young girl who wanted to learn everything as soon as possible.

From the outset, there was something of a "communication gap" between Zalewski and my teenage self. He spoke neither English nor French very well, it seemed; as I knew French ballet vocabulary not at all, I wrote down what his words sounded like: "pirouette" was "pierrette," and that seemed perfectly all right to me; "arasgon" meant "à la seconde;" "broke" meant "passé;" "port de bras" was "corps de bras;" "chuck" was apparently a kind of flic-flac, or brush dégagé movement; "sta" turned out to be "jeté." My descriptions of the simplest steps that he gave me were completely illiterate, but really quite amusing. It was a long time before I really knew the names of the steps. The importance of vocabulary becomes clear when working with a choreographer or a teacher who only names steps and combinations, without demonstration. Today, dance is scientific, so that young dancers begin to learn the names along with the steps, correctly, from the beginning.

CLASSWORK: JAN ZALEWSKI, INDIANAPOLIS, 1915

Center	Port de Bras
5th pos, R ft front	
Relevé on L ft demi-pte, R ft dégagé écarté	R arm en haut
Tombé on R ft, pas de bourrée (L-R-L)	
Hold 5th pos, L ft front	
Pte-tendue R à la seconde	
Pas de bourrée (R back-L-R)	
Plié in 5th pos	
Pirouette en attitude to R, L ft back	
Plié, pas de bourrée (L-R-L)	
Finish 5th pos, L ft front	
Repeat to other side	

5th pos, R ft front
Relevé on L ft demi-pte
Lift R leg à la seconde
Slowly promenade L into 1st arabesque
Plié, lower R leg into 5th pos, L ft front
Repeat to other side

5th pos, R ft front
Relevé on L ft demi-pte

Center	Port de Bras

Center

Lift R leg éffacé — R arm en haut, éffacé
Tombé on R ft, pas de bourrée (L-R-L)
Plié, L ft front (4th pos croisé)
Pirouette R
Finish 5th pos, R ft back
Repeat to other side, immediately

(Adagio)
5th pos, R ft front
Développé with R leg éffacé
Plié on L ft, tombé on R ft
Slow promenade on R ft, into 1st arabesque
Tap L ft en arrière and lift it
    into attitude croisé
Promenade L en dedans on R ft, one turn
Bend fwd, stretching L attitude into
    arabesque penchée
Throw body back into quick pas de
    bourrée to L ft front croisé
Pirouette en dehors, finish 5th pos,
    L ft front
Repeat to L

5th pos, R ft front
Assemblé fwd, with L leg
Piqué on R ft, L leg in attitude — Arms and head thrown back
Assemblé en arrière with L leg
Piqué on L ft, R leg in passé
Close R ft back in 5th pos
4 sissonnes (ciseaux) fermées (L-R-L-R)
Finish 5th pos, L ft front
Repeat to other side

5th pos, R ft back, facing diag fwd R — Arms 5th en haut
Jump onto R ft, lift L leg back retiré
Tombé on L ft, plié, pas de bourrée en
    tournant (R-L-R)
Pas de bourrée (L-R-L)
Plié, 5th pos, L ft front
Double pirouette from 5th pos (to L on R ft)
Close L ft back in 5th pos
Repeat to other side

2 échappés
Relevé en attitude R

Center   **Port de Bras**

Relevé en attitude L
Repeat

5th pos, R ft front
Jump on L ft, R leg in low
   2nd pos [temps levé]
Step on R ft, assemblé back with L leg
Échappé and change
Repeat to other side

4th pos, L ft back
Coupé with L ft, plié on R ft
Jeté on L ft, R ft back
Brisé with L ft, landing on R ft back
   in 4th pos
Repeat to same side

5th pos, R ft front
Plié
Entrechat-quatre
2 changements
Plié
Entrechat-six
2 changements

4th pos, L ft tendu back
Pas de bourrée (L-R-L) into 2nd pos
Plié
Brisé, landing on R ft, L in coupé pos
Pas de bourrée into 2nd pos
Brisé, landing on R ft
Pas de bourrée back (L-R-L) into 2nd pos
Brisé, landing on L ft
2 jetés (1 jeté if repeating to same side)
Repeat to other side

(Ballotté)
5th pos, R ft front
Plié, relevé
Turn slowly in bourrée to R into
   éffacé pos
Deep plié on L ft, lifting R leg éffacé
Bring R leg slowly down to pte-tendue,
   then into 5th pos soussus

Center

Come down from demi-ptes
Stand on R ft, lift L leg in back
Développé with L leg diag back, plié on R ft
Point L ft tendu, bring into 5th pos,
    rising into soussus
Développé à la seconde with R leg en face
Close 5th pos, R ft back
Then battement rond de jambe (front-side-back)
    with L leg
Plié in 5th pos
Changement
Repeat to other side

5th pos, R ft front
Double pirouette, finish à la seconde
4th pos, R leg back en attitude
À la seconde, 2 ronds de jambe en l'air
Attitude renversé, then kick straight out
    à la seconde
Close R ft back

4th pos, R ft back
Pas de bourrée en tournant en dedans L
Plié, bring L ft around in grand rond de
    jambe à terre to 4th pos front
Plié, double pirouette en dedans L
Finish 4th pos, L ft back
Repeat to other side

5th pos, R ft front
Assemblé fwd with L leg
Relevé in arabesque on L ft
Close 5th pos, R ft back
Repeat with R ft
3 jetés
Brisé
Repeat from 5th pos, L ft front

5th pos, R ft back
2 jetés (R-L)
Assemblé fwd with R leg
Attitude front in relevé on L ft
Close 5th pos, L ft back
Repeat

Port de Bras

Arms 5th en haut and
torso bent to L

Adolph Bolm

ADOLPH BOLM 1884-1951

Adolph Bolm, who was born and reared in St. Petersburg, enjoyed a brilliant career as a leading dancer with Diaghilev's Ballets Russes. He became one of the major influences in laying the foundation of twentieth-century American ballet.

At the Maryinsky Imperial Theatre Ballet School, Bolm studied with Platon Karsavin and Nicholas Legat, graduating in May 1903 with first honors not only in dance, but in music, art, and literature as well. The same year, he partnered Alexandra Baldina in tours through Europe. Returning to Russia, he became a member of the Maryinsky Imperial Ballet and studied with Enrico Cecchetti. Between 1908 and 1910, he danced throughout Europe, partnering Anna Pavlova, and at London's Empire Theatre with Lydia Kyasht.

In May 1909, Bolm made his debut with Diaghilev's Ballets Russes, taking Paris by storm with his performance as the Chief Warrior in Michel Fokine's *Prince Igor.* His superb characterizations in successive Fokine ballets—Pierrot in *Le Carnaval* (1910), the Moor in *Petruchka* (1911), Prince Ivan in *The Firebird* (1910), King Dodon in *Le Coq d'Or* (1914) —increased his popularity.

He permanently joined the Ballets Russes as premier danseur, subsequently becoming ballet master and choreographer, after resigning from the Maryinsky in 1911. He came to America with Diaghilev's company on both its United States tours (1916 and 1917), and was largely responsible for rehearsing its repertoire. While recuperating from an injury on the second tour, Bolm decided to remain in the United States. Shortly thereafter, he founded his Ballet Intime company, which soon disbanded but was revived a few years later. Between 1917 and 1924, he concentrated his efforts in New York, choreographing musical revues (e.g., *Miss 1917,* with seventeen-year-old Ruth Page in the corps de ballet); ballets for the Metropolitan, Chicago, and Colon Operas; and ballet prologues preceding feature films at the Rivoli, Rialto, and Strand Theatres.

In 1919, he choreographed *The Birthday of the Infanta* for the Chicago Opera. It starred Ruth Page, who remained his première danseuse in New York, London, and Chicago until 1927. Bolm moved his school and company to Chicago in 1923, where his choreography became often unconventional, if not innovative. In 1931, he was called to Hollywood to choreograph films. He remained there until his death.

Of his teaching, Ruth Page said in a 1920 interview, "Though he is an intense believer in the necessity of a fundamental technique . . . he is fully in sympathy with the newer tendencies of the ballet." In his school, he used the method of passing his students progressively from one teacher to another. Crediting Bolm's enormous influence in America, critic Ann Barzel said in a 1952 eulogy that he left his mark on countless dancers through "his wide interest in all the arts and his very manly style, especially in character dances."

Adolph Bolm was a graduate of the Imperial Ballet School in St. Peters-burg, but I doubt if he was ever a great classical dancer. His forte was so-called character dancing; his greatest role that of the Chief Warrior in Fokine's Prince Igor. *No one ever excelled him (not even Nureyev) in the excitement he generated in this part. He was also notable as the Moor in* Petruchka *(I danced the Ballerina opposite him), as Pierrot in* Carnaval, *and, much later, as King Dodon in* Coq d'Or *(I used to love to come out of the tent as the Queen of Shemakhan and dance for Bolm in his guise as the doddering old fool he made so amusing).*

My association with Bolm started almost at the beginning of my career. When I came to New York to "finishing" school, I started classes with Bolm. Every day, I went to his studio at 15 East 59th Street—with a chaperone. Since I was alone in New York and the same age as Bolm's stepdaughter, Valitchka, I was soon taken under the Bolms' wing, which was a great experience. Even while babysitting for their young son Olaf, I could listen to Prokofiev practice piano, in person.

I do not think Bolm was ever deeply interested in teaching. His main concerns were performing, making ballets, and establishing his company, the Ballet Intime. Consequently, except for character classes, he was a rather "lazy" teacher. So that he would not have to do all the tedious work of correcting, Bolm, unlike so many other teachers, insisted that I go to other teachers, like Alexis Tarasoff, Aurora Arriaza, and especially Enrico Cecchetti. I had never even heard of Cecchetti until I went to London with Bolm [in 1920] as the première danseuse of his Ballet In-time, performing two shows a day at the Coliseum.

There were many things I learned in those early years from Bolm; he was interested in everything and everybody. He was a great talker, an avid reader, and an informed musician—a man of the world, not just a dancer. But technique was not his strong point. He would talk all through the barre *of his class, doing petits battements with turned-in feet, saying, "Rootie, did you enjoy that music last night? I would love to make ballet to," as if I had already acquired all the technique I needed and knew all I needed to know. But I struggled along, trying to do everything perfectly and writing down many of his steps.*

In class, Bolm took all kinds of liberties and was never strictly classical. He gave marvelous combinations that were always interesting, musical, and different every day. His barre *was short and incorrect, but his center work was very creative, sometimes to the point of awkwardness. He often drove the pianist mad by switching tempos in mid-combination. But, in his approach, Bolm was interested above all in movement, in making* you *dance.*

Of course, Bolm's specialty was character dance, and I was lucky to be in that class. Ironically, in all my notes on his classes, there are only passing mentions of the obertases, mazurkas, Hungarian and Roumanian rhapsodies, hornpipes, gigues, and even ballroom dances like menuets and gavottes that he taught. These lessons were very helpful to me when I had to choreograph so many incidental dances for the various Chicago Opera companies.

Bolm was certainly instrumental in my career, early on giving me starring roles in his ballets, which were not innovative like Fokine's but staged so well. He also encouraged me to create my first choreographies. I was with Bolm so long, and was so influenced by his "Russian-ness," that I almost felt Russian myself. Russians are possessive by nature, I think, and I am sure that Bolm came to think of me as "his." My parents felt that he held me down to a certain extent, and perhaps they were right.

The time for a break was inevitable. It finally happened when I, alone, was invited to perform at the coronation ceremonies of Emperor Hirohito in Japan in 1928. Bolm was outraged and did not have anything to do with me for several years. But artistic blood is thicker than water, I suppose. After a while, when Bolm was happily living, teaching, and creating in California (which all Russians considered the Promised Land), we reconciled. I even took classes with him again when I visited California. I think I was very privileged to have had such a special association with this great, inspiring, and unique man in the history of ballet in our time.

CLASSWORK: ADOLPH BOLM, NEW YORK, 1917

Center	Port de Bras
5th pos, R ft front	
Pas de bourrée dessus en tournant (L-R-L) to R	
Grand battement à la seconde with R leg, then rond de jambe with R leg	Arms 5th en haut
Temps levé on L ft, doing pas de bourrée en tournant en dehors (R-L-R)	
Close 5th pos, R ft front	
Piqué on R ft quickly, L leg à la seconde	
Assemblé en arriére with L leg	
Changement	
Repeat to other side	

Center	Port de Bras

5th pos, L ft back, from C2
Step way back on L ft demi-pte into   R arm en haut
  attitude with R (plié on L)
Step way back on R ft demi-pte into   L arm in 3rd
  arabesque with L (plié on R)
Assemblé soutenu   Arms 5th en haut
Finish 5th pos, R ft back   Look back to R
Repeat to other side from C1

(Waltz)
5th pos, R ft front
Cabriole éffacé on L ft   R arm 5th en haut
Balancé R in place
Relevé on L ft into attitude turn en
  dedans
Cours de pointes [bourrée] in circle
  to L
Repeat to other side

5th pos, R ft front
3 brisés (back to front)
1 assemblé battu (front to back)
Soussus   Arms 5th en haut
Repeat to other side

5th pos, L ft back
Brisé, landing on L ft, R croisé to
  L (brisé volé)
Brisé with R (front to back), landing
  on L (R ft back, coupé pos)
Jeté en avant on R ft
Brisé fwd, landing in 5th pos, R ft
  front
Repeat, same side

(Grand Jeté en Tournant Step)
4th pos, R ft pte-tendue back,
  from C2
Glissade, grand jeté en tournant
Plié, relevé in 1st arabesque   Flutter L hand
Repeat, same side

5th pos, R ft back
Jeté R, landing L ft in front jeté pos   Bend over to side

Center	Port de Bras
Relevé on R ft, développé écarté with L leg	L arm 5th écarté
Tombé onto L ft, pas de bourrée dessous L (R-L-R)	
Repeat to other side	

5th pos, R ft back
Assemblé fwd with R leg — L arm 5th en haut
Temps levé on R ft, L in back jeté pos — L arm en avant
Repeat to L — Arms reversed
Plié, sissonne L, R leg 2nd pos
Pas de bourrée dessous L (R-L-R)
Assemblé en avant with R leg
Repeat to other side
En arrière
Do just the same going back, only end
  temps levé with ft in front jeté pos
  and pas de bourrée dessus

5th pos, R ft front
Battement fondu à la seconde with R ft,
  plié on L ft
Relevé on L ft, 3 ronds de jambe en
  l'air with R leg
Battement fondu and développé with R
  leg croisé L, relevé on L ft
Tombé on R ft, développé à la seconde
  with L leg
Repeat to other side
En Arrière
5th pos, R ft back

Battement fondu with R leg en arrière
Rond de jambe en dedans with R leg
Battement fondu with R leg, relevé on
  L ft, attitude croisé with R leg
Tombé *back* onto R ft and développé L
  leg à la seconde

5th pos, R ft front
Glissade to R, cabriole éffacé on L ft,
  holding R leg up
Plié, close 5th pos, R ft back
Assemblé fwd with R leg

Center	**Port de Bras**

Sissonne fermée, closing L ft front in
    5th pos

5th pos, R ft front
Pas de bourrée couru diag fwd R   R arm 5th en haut
3 temps levé on R ft, cabriole en arrière
Pas de bourrée dessous R (L-R-L)
Pas de bourrée couru diag fwd R
Assemblé, closing L ft front in 5th pos
Pas de bourrée couru diag back L into
    grand jeté en tournant (finish L leg
    in arabesque)
Close 5th pos, L ft front
Repeat to R (point fwd and begin with pas
    de bourrée couru diag fwd L)

4th pos éffacé, R ft pte-tendu
    back
Pas de bourrée couru diag fwd R into   R arm 5th en haut
    grand jeté onto R ft
Relevé on R ft, failli with L to croisé   L arm 5th en haut
Close 5th pos, L ft front   R arm 3rd en avant
Assemblé fwd with R leg
Jeté L   L arm 3rd en avant
Step onto R ft   R arm 3rd en avant
Repeat to other side

5th pos, R ft back
Jeté R, doing rond de jambe en l'air
    en dedans with L leg
Close 5th pos, L ft front
Assemblé fwd with R leg
Assemblé back with R leg
Repeat to other side

(Adagio)
5th pos, R ft front
Plié
Double pirouette en dehors, finish R ft   L arm 5th en haut
    croisé front
Promenade on L ft to L, bringing R leg
    into attitude en arrière, finish en face   Arms 4th, L en haut
Bend way over to L
Straighten up quickly, bringing R leg
    à la seconde

Center	Port de Bras

2 ronds de jambe en l'air en dehors
   with R leg, swing R leg into flic-flac
   L, finish R leg à la seconde
Pas de bourrée en tournant en dehors
   (R-L-R)
Assemblé soutenu
Repeat to other side

5th pos, R ft front
Pas de bourrée en tournant (L-R-L),
   finish R ft in front jeté pos
2 pas de chats to R   Arms pointing up to R
Soussus   Arms 5th en haut

4th pos, R ft pte-tendue back
Brisé R, finish L ft croisé front
   (brisé volé)
Jeté (small leap) L on L ft (croisé)
Brisé (front to back), finish 5th pos,
   R ft back
Pas de chat (lifting R ft first), finish
   5th pos, L ft front
Repeat to other side

(Adagio)
5th pos, R ft back
Glissade sans change to R
Step onto R ft into double pirouette en   R arm fwd, 1st arabesque
   arabesque, finish facing R and hold
   arabesque
Plié on R ft
Quarter turn (promenade) slowly into éffacé,   Change to L arm fwd
   bending back R   R arm en haut
Petit battement with L ft at R ankle
Attitude with L leg, relevé on R ft
Plié in 4th pos, L ft front croisé, grand port
   de bras
Attitude with L leg
Deep plié on R ft and développé with L leg
   into 3rd arabesque   L arm croisé
Straighten R knee, close soussus,
   L ft front
Open into 4th pos, R ft back, plié
Pirouette à la seconde en dedans

	Center	Port de Bras

Center	Port de Bras
Pull R ft into passé pos for double pirouette en dedans	
Finish 5th pos, R ft front	
Glissade sans change to L and repeat to other side	
5th pos, R ft back	
Assemblé fwd with R leg	
Assemblé back with R leg	
Sissonne ouverte into arabesque croisé to R	L arm en haut
Assemblé en arrière into 5th pos, R ft back	
Plié, single pirouette en l'air, landing 5th pos, R ft front	Arms 5th en haut
Repeat to other side	
En Arrière	
5th pos, R ft front	
Assemblé back with R leg	
Assemblé fwd with R leg	
Sissonne ouverte en arrière onto L ft, R leg fwd éffacé	L arm en haut
Assemblé en avant into 5th pos, R ft front	
Plié, single pirouette en l'air, landing 5th pos, R ft back	
5th pos, R ft front	
Échappé into 2nd pos plié	
Temps levé in 2nd pos, échappé, close 5th pos sans change (in one count)	
Jeté L, R ft coupé front	
Assemblé back with R leg, soussus, plié	
Entrechat-quatre, finish 5th pos, L ft front	
Repeat to other side	

CHICAGO, SEPTEMBER 25, 1924

Center	Port de Bras
5th pos, R ft front	Arms 1st
Jeté L, R ft front	
Plié on L ft, R leg attitude en avant	

Center	Port de Bras
Relevé on L leg, développé R leg croisé	L arm en haut
Plié, relevé and développé R leg éffacé (balançoire back)	
Plié, relevé and arabesque with R leg croisé	R arm en bas
Plié and pas de bourrée dessus L (R-L-R)	Lift R arm gradually into 5th en haut
Repeat to other side	Arms 1st

(Waltz)	
5th pos, R ft front	
Balancé diag fwd R on R ft	R arm en haut, L en bas
Balancé diag back on L ft	R arm en bas
Glissade diag fwd R, grand jeté on R ft	R arm en avant
Piqué on L ft and one attitude turn L	R arm en haut
Step onto R ft, plié, assemblé fwd with L leg	
Temps levé in 5th pos, moving back	Arms 2nd
Repeat to other side	

5th pos, R ft front	
Step on R ft demi-pte, L leg in arabesque	Swing R arm in circle across front, repeat with L arm
Plié	Arms diag fwd L
2 steps (L-R) diag fwd R, grand jeté onto L ft	Arms 5th en avant
Step back on R ft, glissade back	
Cabriole en arrière éffacé	
Step onto L ft, plié, petit battement with R ft	
Finish in relevé on L demi-pte, R ft low passé back	Arms diag fwd L

("Semi-Greek")	
2 hops on R ft, L ft croisé front (rather high)	R arm en bas, pointing toward L ft; L arm high, pointing diag back L
2 hops on L ft, R leg en attitude	Arms diag fwd R
Promenade half turn	
Hop on R ft, L leg en attitude croisé	Arms in same pos; head facing diag fwd R
Hop on L ft, R leg sweeping through to arabesque (balançoire)	Arms swing down through 1st and up to diag fwd L

Center	Port de Bras
2 steps (R-L), glissade and big temps levé onto R ft, L leg in 1st arabesque	
Repeat to other side	
5th pos, R ft front	
Jeté battu onto L ft	
Temps levé on L ft, R éffacé	L arm en haut
Temps levé on L ft, bringing R leg into arabesque croisé	R arm en avant
Temps levé, coupé on R ft, 2 ronds de jambe en l'air en dehors with L leg	L arm en haut
Pas de bourrée dessous to R (L-R-L)	
Entrechat-trois, R ft cou-de-pied back	
Repeat to other side	
5th pos, R ft front, from C2	
Glissade diag back L, entrechat-six en tournant, finish 5th pos, R ft back	Arms en bas
2 steps diag fwd (R-L)	
Cabriole croïsé en arrière on L ft	
Glissade back L corner, step, jeté en tournant	Gradually lift L arm, bending wrist back
Ballonné with R leg diag fwd R	Raise R arm en haut
2 steps (R-L), grand jeté onto R ft	L arm en avant
5th pos, R ft back	
2 brisés to R	
Brisé with L ft, finish L ft front jeté pos	R arm en bas
Temps levé on R ft	
Jeté to L éffacé	
Temps levé on L ft	
Jump onto R ft	Arms diag fwd R
Jeté battu en arrière to L	L arm en haut, R en bas
(*"Butterfly Step"*)	
1st pos, for pas de bourrée couru	
Bourrée fwd en face (two counts)	Arms 2nd, move en avant
Bourrée in circle to R (quick)	R arm 5th en haut, and down
Bourrée in circle to L (quick)	L arm 5th en haut
Bourrée back (en arrière)	Lift R arm to L, to arms 5th en haut

Center

(Pizzicato quality)
5th pos, R ft front
Glissade changé to R
Step onto L ft, lifting R leg à la
    seconde, then sharp passé
Close soussus, R ft back
Sharp passé with L leg
Close soussus, L ft back
3 steps (R-L-R)
2 temps levé on L ft, diag fwd L, R
    leg in passé
Come down on R ft, plié
Bourrée diag back L
Repeat to other side

DETROIT, 1925

Center

(Nice circle)
5th pos, R ft front
2 piqué turns on R pte
2 balancés (R-L), low down, covering
    ground
Chaîné turns R (two counts)
Grand jeté on R ft
Repeat, completing large circle

5th pos, R ft front in jeté pos
4 emboîtés en tournant R, in straight line
Plié in 5th pos
Small temps levé en tournant on L ft, R
    ft front jeté pos
Coupé with R ft
Cabriole front on R ft
Step on L ft, jeté battu back, finish
    L ft front jeté pos
Repeat to other side

Enrico Cecchetti, London, 1921

ENRICO CECCHETTI
1850-1928

Enrico Cecchetti, developer of what is probably the most influential ballet instruction method of the twentieth century, was born into a family of dancers who then lived in Rome. His teacher, Lepri, was a pupil of Carlo Blasis, the greatest ballet theorist of the nineteenth century, placing Cecchetti in direct connection to the purest classical ballet tradition. As a child, Enrico Cecchetti toured the United States and the capitals of Europe with his family.

Following his debut in St. Petersburg, Russia, in 1887, he stayed and became ballet master to the Imperial Theatre in 1890 (creating the roles of Carabosse and the Bluebird in *The Sleeping Beauty* in the same year). His legendary teaching career in the Imperial Theatre School began in 1892 and lasted until 1910, when he accepted the position of ballet master to Diaghilev's Ballets Russes. Cecchetti opened a school in London in 1918, and it was there that he first taught Ruth Page, in 1920. In 1923, he returned to Italy to head the ballet school of Teatro alla Scala in Milan, and taught there until his death.

Cecchetti's style and method have been fully documented. The Imperial Society of Teachers of Dancing, an outgrowth of the Cecchetti Society, was founded in London in 1924, and the Cecchetti Council of America was formed in 1939 to preserve the Maestro's system. A selective list of Cecchetti's pupils in Russia and Europe is ample testimony to his unchallenged position as the greatest ballet teacher of the century: Mathilde Kschessinska, Olga Preobrajenska, Lubov Egorova, Vera Trefilova, Agrippina Vaganova, Anna Pavlova, Nicholas Legat, Michel Fokine, Vaslav Nijinsky, Adolph Bolm, Lydia Lopokova, Tamara Karsavina, Anatole Oboukhoff, Leonide Massine, Alicia Markova, Anton Dolin, Cia Fornaroli, Luigi Albertieri, Vincenzo Celli, and Ruth Page.

I always think of Maestro Cecchetti as a very old man. He taught seated in a chair and pounding with his stick on the floor as he sang. He always seemed to be bending over and looking down, but he never missed a trick; if you did anything incorrectly, he would throw his stick at you. After the "set class" (one syllabus for Mondays, another for Tuesdays, and so forth) he gave what he called "temps à plaisir" steps that differed from day to day.

I first studied with Cecchetti in professional class, when I was performing with Adolph Bolm at London's Coliseum in 1920. After barre, *we stood in a circle. Each day we moved up a notch so that the same people would not always be in front. It was a good idea, since it was fair to everyone. It is said that Cecchetti stressed the legs more than the arms, but I thought just the contrary: he was even more exacting with the arms than with the legs. His* port de bras, *although very correctly placed, were always very fluid.*

The second time I studied with Cecchetti was in Monte Carlo. Alicia Markova, Vincenzo Celli, Chester Hale, and I had a class with Maestro every morning at 9 A.M. That was in 1925, and, realizing how valuable these classes were, I wrote down each lesson very carefully. Since then, Cyril W. Beaumont, first with Stanislas Idzikowski and later with Margaret Craske, published the lessons with illustrations, so that the Cecchetti method is recorded forever and readily available.

Before and after every class, all the female pupils had to kiss Maestro on each cheek. My mother, who was with me in London, did not like this idea at all, thinking his cheeks must be covered with germs from all those people's kisses. However, I survived. When Diaghilev came to see our class in 1925, he immediately asked me to join his company. I was on my honeymoon at the time, but I was so surprised to be asked to join the Ballets Russes that I accepted. My new husband had to return to the United States alone.

CLASSWORK: ENRICO CECCHETTI, LONDON, 1920

Center	Port de Bras
(Adagio)	
5th pos, R ft front	
Développé en avant to hip level	L arm en avant
Grand rond de jambe en l'air (front-side-back)	L arm en haut, R arm en avant
Passé and promenade en dehors, finish R leg à la seconde	Arms 5th en haut, bend torso to L
Flic R leg into 1st arabesque	L arm en avant
Relevé, close 5th pos, R ft back	
Repeat to other side	
5th pos, R ft front	
Glissade changé to R	

Center	Port de Bras

Step on R ft into double tour en arabesque R
Plié, pas de bourrée dessous en tournant
    (L-R-L)
Chassé, relevé in attitude croisé on R ft
Plié, opening L leg into arabesque
Pas de bourrée dessous en tournant (L-R-L)
    into 4th pos, R ft pte-tendue back
Close 5th pos, L ft front
Repeat to other side

Center	Port de Bras
5th pos, R ft back, from C2	
Piqué back on R ft, lifting L leg in arabesque croisé	Elbows bent, hands in "prayer" pos front
Piqué back on L ft, lifting R leg in arabesque	Arms 4th, R en haut
Pas de bourrée (R-L-R), jeté en tournant en dehors, finish on L ft	
Assemblé fwd with R leg	
Repeat to other side	

MONTE CARLO, 1925

Center	Port de Bras
(Pas de Mami)	
5th pos, R ft front	Arms 5th en bas
Glissade R	
Double tour en arabesque, finish facing diag fwd R	
Temps levé on R ft, bringing L leg through passé to croisé front	
Plié on R ft	
Temps levé on R ft en tournant, bringing L ft in to R knee (développé tour)	Arms 4th, R en haut
Small temps levé on R ft, L leg in arabesque	
Jump in fouetté en tournant: bring L leg up diag fwd R and swish it completely around turning	
Pas de bourrée dessous R (L-R-L), deep plié on L ft croisé (almost kneel)	

Center	**Port de Bras**
Straighten en tournant R and "throw kiss" diag fwd R	
Pas de bourrée	
Double pirouette and a renversé L	
(Tuesday)	
(Slow tempo)	
5th pos, R ft front	
Pas de bourrée dessous R (L-R-L), pte-tendue with R ft	Arms 5th en bas
Petits battements with R ft on L ankle	
Pte-tendue and repeat petits battements with double beats	
Come down on R ft in plié, pas de bourrée dessous R (L-R-L)	
Flic-flac to L and plié on L ft	Arms 2nd
Pas de bourrée L (R-L-R)	
Pas de chat	
Repeat fast	
(Difficult variation)	
5th pos, R ft front	
Jeté en tournant diag fwd R	
Small assemblé en avant (without straightening knee)	
Temps levé en tournant R on L ft	
1 fouetté en dehors R on L ft	
1 fouetté en dedans R on R ft	
Repeat 3 times, very small	
Move diag back to center with very quick échappés sans changes	
3 relevé pirouettes à la seconde L	
Double pirouette en dedans, L ft back jeté pos	Arms 5th en haut
Repeat 3 times	
Run fwd to C2, finish on L ft, R pte-tendue back éffacé	
2 jetés en tournant	
3 chaîné turns in a circle	
(Effective, difficult wheel)	
4th pos, L ft pte-tendue back	
Dégagé, pas de bourrée en tournant to R	
Grand jeté into 1st arabesque	

Center

For 1st wheel
Coupé jeté with L ft back in attitude,
  jumping high with the accent up

(Effective turn)
(Preparation): Attitude croisé on R ft
Plié, extending L leg into 1st arabesque
Step onto L ft, R leg in arabesque
Hop en tournant in arabesque on L ft
  (keep heel on floor)
Pas de bourrée en tournant
Développé R leg à la seconde
Hop on L ft en tournant
4 relevé turns on L ft, R leg à la
  seconde
Hop for 2 more turns, R leg still à
  la seconde
Plié
Attitude on L ft, doing as many turns
  as possible, with renversé at end

(Thursday)
5th pos, R ft front
Jeté R onto R ft
Relevé on R ft demi-pte ("throw kiss")
Bring L ft down to 5th pos front
Jeté L
Repeat 6 times
Petit jeté fwd croisé on R ft
Assemblé en arrière with L leg, emboîté
  en tournant to R
Plié fwd on R ft in arabesque éffacé R
Pas de bourrée dessous (L-R-L)
Repeat to other side

(Important for elevation)
5th pos, R ft front
Sissonne ouverte on R ft into 1st arabesque
Cabriole en arrière on R ft
Temps levé on R ft
Double cabriole en arrière
Assemblé soutenue
Repeat to other side

Arms from 2nd to 5th
  with each relevé

Constantin Kobeleff, 1926

CONSTANTIN KOBELEFF
1885-1966

Known fondly in his late teaching years in New York as "Koby," Constantin Kobeleff was born in Russia of a "peasant" family. He became a student at the Maryinsky Imperial Ballet School, from which he graduated in 1903 with classmates Alexandra Baldina and Adolph Bolm, a year after Tamara Karsavina, Lydia Kyasht, and Alexandra Fedorova-Fokine (who later also became a widely respected teacher in New York). He joined Diaghilev's Ballets Russes in 1909 and came to the United States with that company in 1916. He remained to become a United States citizen.

In the United States, Kobeleff's dancing career was diverse. Later in life, as a teacher, he stated his belief that ballet was a basis for *all* dancing, which he had proved earlier as a dancer on the Keith and Orpheum vaudeville circuits, with the Chicago Opera Company, as partner to both Albertina Rasch and Anna Pavlova, as premier danseur in *Cinderella* at the New York Winter Garden (1922), and as chief character dancer with Pavlova's company on its last tour of the United States in 1926.

Kobeleff began teaching in 1926 in New York City. Among his students in those first years were some of the most outstanding ballet and show dancers of the period: Ruth Page, Charlotte Greenwood, Anna Ludmilla, Vlasta Maslova, and Queenie Smith (the original star of Gershwin's *Tip Toes*). In the 1940s, Kobeleff taught primarily at the Albertina Rasch studio, and continued to teach in New York until he retired in 1960.

Some sources claim that Kobeleff taught the Cecchetti method. However, it is more likely that, having departed from the Maryinsky-Cecchetti influence so early in his career, he taught a method of his own. Advertisements for his classes promised a method of ballet instruction "as suitable to musical comedy as it is to the concert stage and the opera."

Kobeleff openly admitted the superiority over other nationalities of American female dancers, praising them as quick learners, full of "energy, pep and intelligence," though a little too ambitious. His widespread popularity and influence were undoubtedly enhanced by "Normal" courses offered annually for teachers from throughout the United States and Europe. Several years after his retirement, Koby suffered a broken hip, from which he never recovered. He died at Knickerbocker Hospital in New York.

Kobeleff was one of Bolm's many assistant teachers. I remember his classes with pleasure because they were so "dancey." I probably learned very little about developing my own technique because Kobeleff rarely corrected. But he kept us jumping and flying around so fast, we must at least have built up our stamina. Kobeleff seemed to be clearly a product of the St. Petersburg school; he taught what we thought of, at the time, as typically Russian ballet classes. I did not study with Kobeleff for any prolonged time, but I did write down what I thought were some of his more interesting combinations.

CLASSWORK: CONSTANTIN KOBELEFF, NEW YORK, 1924

Center	Port de Bras
(Waltz time)	
5th pos, R ft front	
Balancé diag fwd R, coupé dessous with L ft	
Cabriole en tournant on R ft, finish facing C1	Arms 4th, R arm en haut
Jeté en tournant L, landing on R ft, L leg in arabesque	
Plié on R ft, relevé	
Step onto L ft, R leg in arabesque éffacé	
Jeté onto R ft, close L front	
Relevé, plié (preparation)	
Double tour en l'air en dehors L	
Relevé on L ft, R ft dégagé devant	
Close R ft front	
Assemblé fwd en tournant with L leg	
Finish 5th pos, L ft front	
Repeat to other side	

(Difficult, to pizzicato music)
5th pos, R ft front, facing C1
2 hops on R pte, diag back R
2 hops on L pte, diag fwd L
Pas de bourrée couru en avant eight counts
2 sissonnes fermées en pte
Relevé on L ft en arabesque, coupé back R
Rond de jambe en tournant L

Center	Port de Bras

(Effective combination)
5th pos, R ft front
3 entrechats-six
Relevé on L demi-pte, R ft in sharp   Arms 3rd; look down L
   passé
Close in 5th pos, R ft back
Repeat to other side
2 steps (R-L) diag fwd L
Piqué on R ft in arabesque croisé
2 steps back (L-R)
Piqué on L ft, R in low dégagé croisé
   front
Coupé, R ft over, 2 steps (L-R) en
   tournant
Grand jeté on L ft into arabesque croisé
Glissade sans change, assemblé en arrière
   with R leg
Repeat to other side

(Step to cover ground)
4th pos éffacé, R ft pte-tendue front,
   from C3
3 steps (R-L-R) diag fwd R
Grand jeté onto L ft, R leg attitude
   croisé
Step fwd on R ft, big assemblé fwd with   Arms 5th en haut
   L leg (cover ground)
Glissade R, cabriole éffacé on L ft
Hop on R ft, coupé dessus with L ft   Look down
Cabriole on L ft
Bring R leg down in 2nd pos
Double pirouette en dehors R
Glissade diag back R
Big cabriole croisé on L ft
2 steps (R-L) en tournant L
Grand jeté onto R ft
Pas de bourrée couru straight back
   (cover ground)
Grand jeté en tournant L, finish
   4th pos, L ft front
Double pirouette en dehors
Finish L ft pte-tendue front
Repeat to other side, from C4

Center   Port de Bras

(Very difficult)
Do turns in 2nd pos, bringing ft into
    5th pos each time

(Effective jump)
4th pos, L ft pte-tendue back, from C2
2 steps (L-R), coupé with L ft, jeté en tournant,
    landing on R ft
2 steps fwd (L-R), grand jeté L

_L_UIGI ALBERTIERI _1869-1930_

Luigi Albertieri was considered the last teacher in the great tradition of Italian ballet technique, which was epitomized in the method of Enrico Cecchetti. In fact, Albertieri, born in Italy, was Cecchetti's foster son and, from the age of eight, studied exclusively with the Maestro for ten years. At eighteen, he substituted for his mentor at a moment's notice in the Manzotti spectacle, _Excelsior,_ and a highly successful dancing career was launched.

Albertieri danced in Russia, Spain, France, and England, and was frequently praised by the press for his "multiple pirouettes." In London, he was engaged as _primo ballerino_ and ballet master at the Empire Theatre, partnering Katti Lanner, Malvina Cavallazzi, and Adeline Genée. He subsequently produced and danced in ballets at Covent Garden Opera House for seven years. In 1895, Albertieri was invited to be solo dancer and ballet master at the Metropolitan Opera House, New York; he accepted and held the post for fourteen years. Following his tenure at the Metropolitan, which ended in 1909, he held similar posts with the Chicago, Philadelphia, San Carlo, Manhattan, and Century opera companies until opening his own studio at 11 East 59th Street, New York, in 1915.

For the next fifteen years, Luigi Albertieri's reputation was unrivaled (possibly excepting that of his compatriot, Stefano Mascagno). Advertisements for his school boasted a quotation from Pavlova herself: "By far the best dancing school I know of in America." His students, other than Ruth Page, included Rosina Galli, Maria Gambarelli, Lydia Lopokova, Albertina Rasch, and Fred Astaire. He also coached the actresses Maude Adams, Annette Kellerman, and Mrs. Leslie Carter.

Albertieri taught seated in a chair, accompanying himself on a violin. His command of English was slight, but one pupil stated that when he moved "his feet just a little, I understood more from him than from any other teacher in the world." Diaghilev ballerina Lydia Lopokova (Lady Keynes) compared his teaching method to Cecchetti's: Albertieri was "kinder to the class, more gentle to the pupils ... He was a charming, lovable Italian of the old school—a happy-go-lucky fellow with his violin and Italian cigarettes." Unlike Cecchetti, Lopokova continued, Albertieri was not a "big, fierce character," but, she concluded, "a nice ... gentleman, with traditions and knowledge, but no demon inside him."[3]

Albertieri's book, _The Art of Terpsichore_ (published in 1923), was called "the first of its kind in its precise technical expression ... a catechism of dancing." It cost $10.00—a high price for a book of any kind at the time. Shortly before his death, Albertieri made a sound film, _The Ballet Class,_ "a story of the Degas Era."

---

[3]_Dancing Times,_ December 1930.

Luigi Albertieri

In 1923 and 1924, I was the featured solo dancer in Irving Berlin's second Music Box Revue. Dancing every night and two matinee performances, I needed to keep up my technique. The classes of Luigi Albertieri, which were popular at the time, started at noon and ended at four, but I went to them religiously. I have never attended such a long class anywhere in the world.

Between each section of his class, we did have a long rest. We started with a short, simple barre—*about twenty minutes—then rested at least twenty minutes. We repeated the* barre *in the center, and rested again. The* adagio *section had all the famous Cecchetti* adagios, *including a new one, "Pas de Mami," which he composed on the occasion of the opening of his Academie de Danse in London and named after his cat. Another "intermission" was followed by lots of very fancy pirouettes; I loved this section, since my turns were rather feeble. A long rest, and the class ended, as is usual, with jumps.*

Roughly, Albertieri's classes followed the Cecchetti pattern, with one big difference: Cecchetti's classes were very concise and tight; Albertieri's sprawled out in a leisurely way. Albertieri's steps were decidedly harder, but he never corrected anyone—at least, I do not remember his ever having corrected me. As a personality, Albertieri does not stand out too clearly in my mind because he never even spoke to me, unlike Cecchetti, who made a big fuss over me. Fortunately, I was very conscientious, but everyone needs corrections.

CLASSWORK: LUIGI ALBERTIERI, NEW YORK, 1923

Center	Port de Bras
(Wednesday)	
5th pos, R ft back	
Assemblé fwd with R leg, temps levé on R ft in diag line	
Without putting L ft down, fouetté soutenu in arabesque, finish en attitude on R ft	
Repeat 3 times	
Coupé dessous with L ft, glissade L	Arms 4th, R en haut
Pas de chats all around in a circle L	

Center	**Port de Bras**

Diag fwd R
1 attitude turn on R ft
Double attitude turn
3 fouettés on L ft (1 double)
Repeat 2 times

5th pos, R ft front
4 jetés with ronds de jambe en l'air fwd
   (L-R, L-R)
Pas de bourrée dessous (L-R-L)
Jeté en tournant R, finish 4th pos,
   R ft back
Double pirouette R, finish 5th pos, L ft
   front
Repeat to other side

5th pos, R ft front
Piqué on R demi-pte (diag fwd R)
Step on L ft, rond de jambe en l'air
   en dehors with R leg
Tombé on R ft, plié
Cabriole en arrière on R ft
Pas de bourrée dessous (L-R-L), jeté en
   tournant to R

1 tour en arabesque on R demi-pte   Arms 4th, L arm up
Repeat to other side
Glissade, pas de chats in a circle R
Stop in center for
4 jetés with ronds de jambe en l'air   Bend way down (cambré)
   fwd (R-L, R-L)   each time
2 cabrioles en arrière on R ft
Repeat 4 jetés and 2 cabrioles
Piqué turns in circle (wheel) R

(Nice toe step)
5th pos, R ft front
Relevé on R pte, 2 ronds de jambe
   en l'air with L leg, close 5th
   pos, L ft front
Relevé on L pte, 2 ronds de jambe
   en l'air with R leg, close 5th
   pos, R ft front
Repeat 4 times
4 relevés en pte (L-R-L-R), lifting   Bend way down (cambré)
   working leg à la seconde   each time

Center	Port de Bras
Glissade changé R with R ft	
Bring L leg in front croisé (diag fwd R) in attitude devant (still in relevé on R pte)	
Repeat to other side	
Relevé back on R ft, bringing L leg from front dégagé through passé to arabesque (gradually)	
Fouetté soutenu on L pte 2 times	
Double pirouette en dedans on L ft, finish R leg à la seconde	
Close 5th pos, L ft front	
5th pos, R ft front	
Plié on L ft, R ft pte-tendue side	
Relevé on L ft, R sur le cou-de-pied	Head down and up each time
Repeat once	
Repeat again, bringing R leg into high passé	
Hold as long as possible	
Close 5th pos, R ft back	
Repeat to L	
Repeat to R	
Little pas de bourrées courus en pte ("wiggles") in small circle	Look down; arms 2nd
Repeat 2 relevés	
Little pas de bourrées in circle, then diag fwd R	
2 pas de chats	

Alexandre Volinine in his Paris studio, 1930, with students (André Eglevsky seated on barre, extreme left)

ALEXANDER VOLININE
1882 - 1955

Alexander Volinine was born in Moscow and completed his dance studies there, graduating from the Imperial Bolshoi Theatre Ballet School in 1901. He became a member of the Bolshoi Ballet, was soon elevated to premier danseur, and danced in St. Petersburg as well as in Moscow. Almost immediately, he began to teach at the Imperial Schools of Dance and Drama, where he demonstrated a keen interest in the technical difficulties inherent in classical ballet, and in helping students to surmount them. However, it would be several decades before he could devote his full time to teaching.

In 1910, Volinine took a leave of absence from the Bolshoi in order to accept an invitation to partner Ekaterina Geltzer in performances with Diaghilev's Ballets Russes in Paris. He never returned to Russia, but toured with Adeline Genée in 1912–13, and from 1914 to 1926 was principal partner to Anna Pavlova on her tours of the United States, South America, Europe, the Middle East, and the Far East. After eighteen years of touring, Volinine's desire was to return to teaching. "The idea at the back of my mind," he would say later, "was to devote myself to the teaching side of dancing, while I was still in the flower of my force." He realized his goal in October 1926, when he opened the doors of his Académie d'Art Chorégraphique at 9 Avenue de Montespan in Paris, where he died.

Volinine's studio was a great success from the outset, catering to a select clientele. It was housed in a famous mansion in a stylish quarter of Paris, and was marked by elegance, from the muted tones of the walls and draperies to the parquet floors and large mirrors as well as the immaculate appearance of the students.

Volinine's method of teaching was as muted, yet imposing, as the surroundings. His approach was severe, stressing perfection of line, strenuous toe work (even for boys), and clarity of execution. His ultimate aim was stretching and elongating the body for elegance—hence, his emphasis on stretch work at the *barre*. Volinine's strict, but solicitous, training was reflected in the high caliber of perfection demonstrated by his pupils, a partial list of whom includes André Eglevsky, David Lichine, Tatiana Riabouchinska, Lubov Rostova, Dorothie Littlefield, William Dollar, Jean Babilée, Zizi Jeanmaire, and Leslie Caron.

Alexander Volinine is a somewhat hazy memory for me. I do remember that, as a "jeune fille" in the Pavlova Company, I had a terrible crush on him. I particularly loved his Pierrot solo and his pantomime with the red ribbon. Volinine was not a dynamic, but a charming dancer; his partnering of Pavlova seemed perfection itself.

I was rather surprised to find that he was teaching in Paris in the 1930s, and that the same perfection was revealed in his classes. I was not in class with him long enough to write in detail about his "method," but he seemed to me then to be a very fine teacher with a correct technique.

Volinine's barre *was new to me. It was the first time I had been given* barre *exercises in which you faced toward or away from the* barre. *Now, everyone does class with this kind of stretching exercises, but I have included a few examples of what Volinine was giving in Paris in 1937.*

CLASSWORK: ALEXANDER VOLININE, PARIS, 1937

Barre	**Port de Bras**
Stand back to barre	Both hands on barre
1st pos, feet turned in	
Bend fwd, touch head to knees	
Plié almost to floor	
Straighten legs, then torso	
Stand back to barre	Both hands on barre
5th pos, R ft front	
8 pas de chats, alternating direction	
8 gargoulliades, alternating direction	
("Hitch-kick")	
Stand back to barre	Both hands on barre
4th pos, R ft pte-tendue back	
Grand battement fwd with R leg	
Grand battement fwd with L leg, before bringing R to floor	
Finish in 4th pos, L ft pte-tendue back	
Repeat to other side	
Stand parallel to barre	L hand on barre
Place L ft on barre	
Bend away from barre to R	L arm en haut, R hand on back L hip
	R arm over to L ankle
Bend toward L leg on barre	
Straighten torso	Grand port de bras with R arm (very exagerrated)

Barre

Repeat to other side with R leg

Stand facing barre in 2nd pos
Place R leg on barre à la seconde
Bend to R

Bend to L

Lift R leg off barre, hold à la seconde
    en l'air
Bring R leg back in attitude
Passé, développé devant, placing R
    leg back on barre
Repeat once
Repeat 2 times to other side

(Balançoire)
Stand parallel to barre
Kick straight front with R leg, bring
    back, R ft pte-tendue à terre, deep
    plié on L ft (like lunge)
Kick back with R leg, bring front,
    R ft pte-tendue à terre, knee straight
Relevé on L ft, deep plié
Kick to side with R leg, lower, R ft
    pte-tendue à terre, knee straight
Relevé on L ft, deep plié
Kick back with R leg, bring front,
    deep plié on L ft
Kick front with R leg, bring back, R ft
    pte-tendue à terre, knee straight
Repeat to side, turn
Repeat to other side

Stand back to barre
16 relevés on L ft, R ft sur le cou-de-pied
    back
Repeat, reversing feet

Center

5th pos, R ft front
Pas de bourrée R (L-R-L), assemblé
    en tournant L with R leg
Plié, 4th pos, R ft back

Port de Bras

Both hands on barre

L arm en haut, reaching
    overhead to R
R arm en haut, reaching
    overhead to L

L hand on barre

Both hands on barre

Port de Bras

Center	Port de Bras

Center   **Port de Bras**

Double pirouette en dehors, finish 5th
    pos, R ft back
Relevé on L ft, R leg in arabesque
Close 5th pos, L ft front
Repeat to other side

5th pos, R ft front
Contretemps R
Cabriole en arrière on L ft, finish
    croisé on L ft
2 steps (R-L), Italian saut de basque:
    starting on R ft, kick L leg up diag fwd
    R, turn in air, finish facing diag fwd R
    on L ft, R leg in arabesque croisé
2 steps back (R-L), step on R ft to C3
Cabriole en avant en tournant: hit L
    leg in front of R, turn in air, finish
    facing diag fwd R on L ft croisé
Step on R ft, piqué on L ft, R leg in   Arms 2nd
    1st arabesque
Balance   Arms 5th en haut
Close 5th pos, L ft front

EDNA L. McRAE B. 1901

Edna McRae was born in Chicago, and although widely travelled throughout her career, she chose to endow her hometown with the fruits of her prodigious training and experience. McRae was a graduate of the Chicago Normal School of Physical Education and the Harvard Summer School, but she studied dance with an array of teachers which a formal education could never provide. Her ballet training included studies with Madeline B. Hazlitt, Andreas Pavley, Serge Oukrainsky, Adolph Bolm, Marie Swoboda, Chester Hale, Nicholas Legat, Lubov Egorova, Mathilde Kschessinska, Olga Preobrajenska, Vera Trefilova, and Tamara Karsavina. The famous Cansinos were McRae's instructors in Spanish dancing, and she studied tap dancing with the great John Bubbles.

Although she performed with the Pavley-Oukrainsky Ballet, Bolm's Ballet Intime, and the Chicago Allied Arts, McRae's passion was for teaching. As early as 1920, she was teaching at the Pavley-Oukrainsky School, the Francis Parker School in Chicago, and the Perry-Mansfield Camp in Steamboat Springs, Colorado, where she taught until 1933. In 1923, she opened her own school at 617–618 Lyon and Healy Building, Chicago, offering courses not only in ballet (a carefully graded system), but in character and tap, which she deemed equally important.

For forty years, Edna McRae taught her meticulous classes, striving to develop a "steely" technique in her students, and earned the highest respect from everyone who knew and studied with her. She retired in 1964 from full-time teaching, but continued to guest-teach for years thereafter.

Edna McRae was truly a great teacher, and not sufficiently appreciated by her home town—Chicago. I took classes from Edna rather late in my career, and I was surely grateful to her. Her classes sometimes became a bit boring because they were always geared to the worst pupil, and we all had to wait while the slowpoke was corrected. I used to take Edna's class late in the afternoon after I had been working all day rehearsing at the Opera. I told Edna that I came to her class to relax after a hard day's work, but she never seemed to understand what I meant. After giving instructions, doing choreography, and yelling at my company for six hours, I found it so peaceful to have someone tell me what to do and do the thinking for me. I got a great deal out of Edna's classes; her strictness was just what I needed at the time.

Edna became the ballet mistress for the children in my first year of The Nutcracker *in 1965. She had just retired from full-time teaching, and was thus able to give me all her time. It was a great experience for*

Edna McRae, with pupils

the children of Chicago, who all came from different dance schools, to work with such a great woman. They adored her discipline (the idea that children have to be free to "express" themselves is pretty ridiculous), and danced so correctly and with such feeling that they always made a big hit with the audience. I regret that Edna, now retired, is unable to be with our Nutcracker any longer. Patricia Klekovic, her star pupil and long one of my leading dancers, seems to be carrying on Edna's strict but inspiring method in her children's classes at the Ruth Page Foundation School. But none of us will ever forget Edna, and I am sure that all the children's parents are as grateful to her as I am.

CLASSWORK: EDNA McRAE, CHICAGO, CA. 1942–43

Center

5th pos, R ft front
Petit battement side with R ft, back-
   front sur le cou-de-pied
Sissonne R into 4th pos, L ft croisé
   front
Relevé, attitude turn L on L ft
Plié on L ft, R leg low à la seconde
Relevé on L ft into double développé turn
   en dedans L (R ft in front piqué pos)
Plié on L ft, R leg low à la seconde
Assemblé soutenu en tournant L
Close 5th pos, R ft back
Repeat to other side

5th pos, R ft front
Échappé into 2nd pos
Entrechat-trois, finish R ft back sur le
   cou-de-pied of L
Échappé into 2nd pos
Entrechat-trois, finish L ft back sur le
   cou-de-pied of R
2 petits jetés (L-R)
Échappé into 2nd pos
Double pirouette en dehors R on L ft
Finish 5th pos, R ft back

Center

Repeat to other side
Repeat backward
Entrechat-trois and jetés finish ft front
    sur le cou-de-pied, pirouettes en dedans

EDNA McRAE, CHICAGO, CA. 1964

Barre	**Port de Bras**
(Plié)	
Stand parallel to barre	L hand on barre
1st pos	R arm en bas
Demi-plié, straighten	
Repeat	
Relevé sur les demi-ptes, knees straight	Slowly to 5th en avant
Hold relevé	To 2nd
Lower heels, knees straight	Hold 2nd
Grand plié	Through 5th en bas to en avant
Dégagé R ft à la seconde, pte-tendue	Open to 2nd
Lower heel, 2nd pos à terre	Hold 2nd
Repeat starting in 2nd pos, finish 5th pos, R ft front, after dégagé	To 5th en bas on first demi-plié
Repeat starting in 5th pos, finish 5th pos, R ft front, after dégagé	
Repeat up to grand plié starting in 5th pos	
Demi-plié, 5th pos	R arm en bas
Relevé soussus	To 5th en avant
Hold 6 counts	To 5th en haut, L arm to 5th en haut; both arms to 2nd, palms up
Demi-plié, straighten	Arms 5th en bas
	Hold 5th en bas; head to R over R shoulder (épaulement)
(Battement tendu)	
Stand parallel to barre	L hand on barre
5th pos, R ft front	R arm 2nd
Tendu R ft, 4th pos front, turned out	

Barre	Port de Bras
Barre	**Port de Bras**

Flex ankle and hold
Rotate R leg in and out from hip 2 times
R ft pte-tendue à terre, turned out
Close 5th pos, R ft front
2 battements tendus fwd with R leg
Close 5th pos

Demi-plié, straighten

Repeat en croix (close 5th pos back after first
   tendu to 2nd pos)
Finish demi-plié, straighten

(Port de bras)
Stand parallel to barre
1st pos
Bend body fwd and recover
Bend body back and recover
Hold 1st pos
Repeat double time, adding one more
   fwd bend
Dégagé R ft à la seconde, pte-tendue
Lower R heel, 2nd pos à terre
Bend body L toward barre and recover

Repeat
Bend body R away from barre and recover

Repeat 2 times

Dégagé R ft à la seconde, pte-tendue
Close 5th pos, R ft front
Hold 16 counts

Repeat to other side

(Battement jeté (dégagé, glissé) en balançoire)
Stand parallel to barre

Lift R arm slightly 2nd (breath)
Through 5th en bas, en avant, to 2nd

Both arms 5th en bas; head over R shoulder

L hand on barre
R arm 2nd
Full port de bras

R arm 2nd; look R
Full port de bras, finish R arm 5th en haut

R arm 2nd
R arm inward circle to 5th en haut, then to 2nd

L arm 4th, inward circle to 2nd
Finish both arms 5th en haut
Hold 5th en haut

Inward circle both arms, finish 5th en haut
Repeat
Repeat double time
Lower through 2nd to 5th en bas; head over R shoulder

L hand on barre

Barre	Port de Bras
4th pos, R ft pte-tendue back	R arm 2nd
Small balançoire front and back	
Small balançoire front with relevé, hold	
Reverse, lower L heel on 2 counts	
5 small balançoires alternating front and back	
Small balançoire back in plié on L ft	
Pas de bourrée en dehors R with half turn, finish chassé R ft fwd in plié	
Straighten, L ft 4th pos, pte-tendue back	
Repeat, alternating	

(Rond de jambe à terre)	
Stand parallel to barre	L hand on barre
1st pos	R arm 2nd
Demi rond de jambe	
Point R ft front, dégagé à la seconde, pte-tendue, finish 1st pos	
Repeat	
Repeat to back	
Point R ft front, full rond de jambe en dehors, finish 1st pos	
Demi-plié	En bas
Hold plié on L ft, dégagé R ft to 4th pos, pte-tendue front	En avant
Straighten, dégagé R ft à la seconde, pte-tendue, finish 1st pos	To 2nd
	Hold 2nd
Repeat to back	
Repeat entire exercise	

(Battement frappé)	
Stand parallel to barre	L hand on barre
2nd pos, R ft pte-tendue	R arm 2nd
Place R ft flexed sur le cou-de-pied front	En avant; head L
Piqué [frappé] R ft front, pte-tendue à terre, L ft plié (fondu)	To 2nd; head R
Straighten, R ft flexed sur le cou-de-pied front	En avant; head L
Repeat en croix	

Double frappé battu (back-front) and
    extend à la seconde 4 times
	Through 2nd (or 5th en
	    bas), en avant, to 2nd

Repeat, beats front-back	Repeat

Repeat entire exercise on demi-pte,
    R ft pointed throughout, holding the
    last extension on plié each time for balance	

Barre	Port de Bras

(Rond de jambe en l'air)
Stand parallel to barre
5th pos, R ft front, hold 2 counts
Plié on R ft, L sur le cou-de-pied back
Piqué on L ft, R leg à la seconde
3 ronds de jambe en l'air en dehors,
    finish plié on L ft
Pas de bourrée dessous en dehors (R-L-R)
    quarter turn R, finish plié on R ft,
    L leg low à la seconde
Pas de bourrée dessus en dedans (L-R-L)
    quarter turn R, finish plié on L ft,
    R ft sur le cou-de-pied front
Repeat, facing opposite direction, starting
    3 ronds de jambe en dedans with L leg

Port de Bras:
L hand on barre
R arm 2nd
En bas
To 2nd

Through 5th en avant
   to 2nd

Through 5th en avant to
   5th en bas

R hand on barre

(Battement fondu—Preparation for ballotté)
Stand parallel to barre
5th pos, R ft front, hold 1 count
Demi-plié, relevé soussus
R leg to passé front
Développé R leg to 4th pos front,
    demi-hauteur, L ft plié
Hold plié, lower R ft pte-tendue à terre
Close 5th pos soussus, R ft front
Repeat to back with L leg
Développé R leg à la seconde
Fouetté to arabesque facing barre
Balance in arabesque
Close 5th pos soussus, R ft back,
    facing opposite direction
Repeat to other side

Port de Bras:
L hand on barre
R arm 5th en bas

En avant
To 2nd

En bas

To 5th en haut

Both arms 5th en haut
R hand on barre, L arm
   en bas

(Grand battement)
Stand parallel to barre
5th pos, R ft front
R ft battement tendu front, grand
    battement front
Repeat, finish 4th pos, R ft pte-tendue
    front
Grand battement rond de jambe (battement
    en rond front-side-back), finish 4th
    pos, R ft pte-tendue back

Port de Bras:
L hand on barre
R arm 5th en haut

Barre

Grand battement rond de jambe back-side-
  front, finish 4th pos, R ft pte-tendue front
Grand battement back, finish 5th pos, R ft back
Repeat from beginning, reversing direction
Battement tendu à la seconde, finish 5th pos,
  R ft front
Grand battement à la seconde, finish 5th
  pos, R ft back
Repeat
Grand battement retiré à la seconde, finish
  5th pos, R ft front
Repeat, finish 5th pos, R ft back
Repeat grands battements alternating
  1 time, finish 5th pos, R ft back
Repeat entire exercise, reversing direction

Center	Port de Bras
(Port de bras)	
5th pos en face, R ft front	Arms en bas
Demi plié	
Temps lié with plié to 4th pos front en face	Through 5th en avant to 2nd
Demi-plié in 5th pos	En bas
Repeat to back	
Repeat to R, finish L ft pte-tendue	Through 5th en avant to 2nd
Chassé L ft croisé fwd in plié, lift R leg back	L arm across front
Pas de bourrée dessous (R-L-R), finish in plié on R ft	Through 2nd to R arm across front
Place L ft demi-pte behind R ft, détourné en dehors L (assemblé soutenu en dehors)	Through 5th en avant to 5th en haut
Demi-plié, 5th pos, L ft front	Through 2nd to en bas
Repeat to other side	
(Adagio—Preparation for grand fouetté relevé)	
5th pos croisé, R ft front	Arms en bas
Développé R leg croisé front demi-hauteur, L ft plié	En avant to L across front
Straighten, hold R leg up front	L arm to 3rd
Pivot L to face C3, hold R leg up front	R arm inward to both arms 5th en avant
Turn body over to arabesque croisé with R leg, plié on L ft	R arm front in arabesque

Center	Port de Bras
Finish 5th pos, R ft back	Arms en bas
Développé L leg croisé front	Through en avant to 3rd, R arm en haut
Close 5th pos, L ft front, turning to face C2	Arms en bas
Développé R leg to arabesque éffacé, arabesque penchée, recover	L arm front in arabesque
Relevé in arabesque, tombé on R ft croisé front	R arm across front
Pas de bourrée dessous (R-L-R)	Arms en bas
Finish demi-plié, 5th pos, L ft front, and straighten	
Repeat to other side	

(Battement fondu)

En face, R ft 2nd pos, pte-tendue	Arms 2nd
Battement fondu front with R ft	Through en bas, en avant, to 2nd
Tombé into arabesque plié en face on R ft, relevé	To 2nd
Tombé back on L ft, R sur le cou-de-pied front	En bas
Développé à la seconde demi-hauteur with R leg	To 2nd
Lower R ft, plié in 2nd pos	R arm across front
Pirouette en dehors R, finish demi-plié 5th pos, L ft front	En avant
Straighten, point L ft à la seconde	To 2nd
Repeat to other side	

(Grand fouetté relevé)

Lunge, R ft croisé front	R arm across front
Pirouette en dedans R	To 5th en avant
Dégagé L ft croisé front, R ft plié	Across front
Hold L ft, relevé on R ft	To 3rd
Quick turn on R ft demi-pte to arabesque croisé facing C2, plié on R ft	Inward to 5th en haut; L arm fwd in arabesque
Pas de bourrée dessous (L-R-L) to lunge, L ft croisé front	2nd to L arm across front
Repeat to other side	

Allegro	Port de Bras
5th pos, R ft front	Arms en bas
3 quick jumps in 1st pos, hold	
Repeat	
3 quick jumps in 2nd pos, hold	To 2nd

Allegro	Port de Bras
Repeat	
3 quick changements from 5th pos, R ft front, hold	Inward to 5th en haut
3 quick changements from 5th pos, L ft front, hold	
4 changements (royales)	Outward circle to 5th en bas
Repeat, alternating	
5th pos, R ft front	Arms en bas
Failli R	"Breathe" to demi-2nd
Temps de cuisse R	R arm across front
Failli R, finish R ft sur le cou-de-pied back	L arm across front
Coupé on R ft, assemblé back with L leg	Arms 2nd to en bas
3 entrechats-quatre, 1 royale	
Repeat, alternating	
5th pos, R ft front, near C3	R arm across front
Jeté emboîté en tournant quarter turn R onto R ft	Both arms to 2nd
Repeat, three-quarter turn R onto L ft	R arm across front
Temps levé on L ft, R up in front	
Repeat all	
2 sauts de basque R	Both arms 5th en avant
Quick temps levé on L ft, R up in front	
Chassé R on R ft	To 2nd
Pas de bourrée dessous (L-R-L), finish demi-plié 5th pos, L ft front	L arm across front
Repeat, alternating	

BENTLEY STONE B. 1907

One of the great American male ballet dancers and teachers, Bentley Stone was born in Plankinton, South Dakota. He studied ballet with Margaret Severn, Luigi Albertieri, Laurent Novikoff, and Marie Rambert. His earliest dance performances included appearances in Broadway musicals and the 1929 revival of the 1865 extravaganza, *The Black Crook,* in Hoboken, New Jersey.

Stone went to Chicago, where he became a soloist with the Chicago Civic Opera (1930–32), and from 1933 to 1937 premier danseur and frequent partner of Ruth Page with the subsequent Chicago Opera companies. After a brief association with Ballet Rambert in England in 1937, he returned to Chicago to share directorial, choreographic, and dancing duties with Ruth Page in the Dance Project of Chicago's WPA-funded Federal Theatre Project. Together, they co-choreographed and danced in *American Pattern* (1937), *Frankie and Johnny* (1938), and *Guns and Castanets* (1939). Between 1938 and 1941, they also toured with their own Page-Stone Ballet, choreographing and performing solos, duets, and group works, and in 1941–42 appeared together at the Rainbow Room in New York.

After World War II service, Bentley Stone resumed his partnership with Ruth Page, continuing well into the 1950s, but devoted more time to the Stone-Camryn School, which he had founded with Walter Camryn in 1940. Stone refined his teaching skills over decades and, with Camyrn, produced a number of exceptional dancers. Stone and Camryn closed their school in the spring of 1981 after forty outstanding years.

My long-time partner, Bentley Stone, was a great dancer and is a great teacher. Like me, he is not a "pusher" who knows how to sell himself, a quality so often needed, unfortunately, in the world of dance today. Bentley had an excellent classical training, but I think his technique, so perfect in every detail, was more an expression of himself and his neat mind than a result of his studies. In those days, we scorned the classical ballets and were only interested in creating works that were new and different. Our pas de deux, Tristan and Isolde, *was pure "modern" dance, with heavy plastique that seemed to emanate from Wagner's great music. On the other hand, our dance* Zephyr and Flora, *to Liszt, showed Bentley's extraordinary technique. Although this pas de deux was a satire on classical dancing, which revealed his wry sense of humor, he executed all the positions and* batterie *to perfection.*

Bentley Stone

Bentley started teaching when he was very young in order to make a living. Even though we did many, many well-paid coast-to-coast tours with the Page-Stone Ballet, they still did not keep him busy year-round. While on tour, Bentley gave very careful, wonderful company classes. Finally, he and Walter Camryn started their own school in Chicago. Bentley's classes are very technical, but at the same time very flowing and graceful. Above all, they are intellectual: a student really has to think as well as do in his class. Even I, who knew his work so well, sometimes had difficulty in picking up quickly his intricate steps. Oddly, in the nearly thirty years I worked with Bentley, I took only a few notes on his unique classes. We worked in such close and constant collaboration, I probably saw no need for them. Dolores Lipinski, one of my long-time principal dancers, had her entire training in the Stone-Camryn School. She is a perfect representative of the solid technical foundation their school produced and the only person I know completely capable of continuing their method.

CLASSWORK: BENTLEY STONE, CHICAGO, 1938

Center	Port de Bras
(Adagio)	
5th pos, R ft front	Arms 5th en haut
1 slow assemblé en tournant R, putting L ft in front of R in 5th pos	Look down
Put R ft sur le cou-de-pied back, face C1	Arms en bas
Développé diag fwd R	
Relevé on L ft demi-pte	L arm en haut
Plié on L ft, bend fwd over R leg	
Développé R leg diag back R into arabesque croisé, face C2	R arm diag fwd L
Grand battement with R leg diag fwd L, lower in 4th pos à terre	
2 promenades R on R ft, L leg à la seconde	
Coupé L ft, attitude with R leg	
1 promenade en attitude, finish R ft front sur le cou-de-pied	
Quick glissade into arabesque on R ft	Arms low 2nd
Relevé in arabesque on R ft	L arm en haut

Center	Port de Bras
Développé L leg diag fwd R (croisé)	
Step diag fwd R on L ft	Arms 5th en haut
R ft sur le cou-de-pied back, R leg into high arabesque allongée	
Step back on R ft, close L ft through 1st pos and step back on it into arabesque allongée with R leg	
Bring R ft into 5th pos	
4th pos, L ft front	
Double pirouette en dehors R, finish in 4th pos	Arms 2nd
Repeat pirouettes	
Kneel on R knee, bend fwd over raised L knee	
Stand, weight on L ft, R ft pte-tendue back croisé, facing diag fwd R	Arms diag fwd R

CHICAGO, 1946

Center	Port de Bras
(Waltz)	
5th pos, R ft front	
Balancé en tournant R, repeat L	
Plié on R ft, L in low passé pos back,	
Coupé L ft, hitch-kick front (R-L), finish on R ft, L pte-tendue front croisé	
Balancé on L ft to C1 with half turn R (back to public)	
Plié, R ft front croisé, L low passé pos back	
Coupé L ft, relevé on L ft, R leg battement rond de jambe (front-side-back)	
Glissade R, step on R ft	
Jeté en tournant, finish on L ft	R arm en haut
Grand jeté, half turn R, finish croisé on R ft	
Relevé on R ft in 3rd arabesque	
Glissade en tour L, step on L ft	
Grand jeté R, finish on R ft	
2 steps (L-R)	
Grand jeté, finish croisé on L ft	
(Circular arms)	
5th pos, R ft front	

Center	Port de Bras
Relevé on R ft, L leg in arabesque	Circle both arms, R-over-L, finish both arms R
Glissade L to high 3rd arabesque on L ft, leaning L	
Glissade to R, step on R ft (little lunge)	
2 stepover turns en dehors to R on L ft, ending 3rd arabesque plié on L ft	
Glissade R, half turn L, piqué to soussus (R ft front)	Arms through 2nd to 5th en haut, turn hands in at last moment
Go diag fwd R	
Plié on R ft, jeté on L ft (back hitch-kick running)	
Repeat with grand jeté, finish on L ft	
Glissade back (starting R ft) into grand jeté en tournant, finish on L ft	
Balancé R	
Piqué to high 3rd arabesque on L ft	
Repeat to other side	
(Effective jump)	
5th pos, R ft front	
Sissonne R, coupé on L ft	
Ballonné R, sissonne R, coupé on L ft	L arm croisé en avant
Battement rond de jambe (front-side-back)	Bring R arm to 3rd arabesque
Glissade croisé diag back R	
Step on R ft, relevé and inside développé turn R, finish R in 3rd arabesque, facing C2	
Bring L ft to low passé pos back, temps levé on R ft	
Temps levé on L ft in 3rd arabesque	
Glissade diag back R	
Relevé into attitude turn R	
Coupé L ft, step R-L to C2	
Kick R leg front croisé (knee straight)	L arm 2nd (but a little to front near R leg)
Temps levé on L ft, balançoire with R ft to back	Change R arm to front 4th arabesque croisé)
Glissade, step, hop on R ft in arabesque	Both arms en bas
Glissade, assemblé fwd	

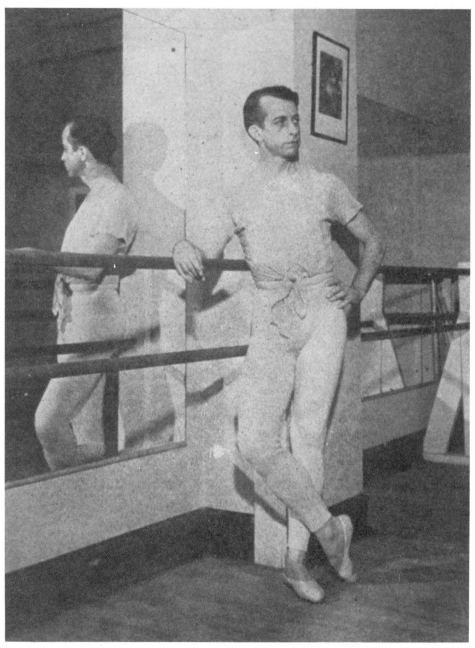

Walter Camryn in his studio at the Stone-Camryn School, 1945.
Photo by Ann Barzel

WALTER CAMRYN B. 1903

Born in Helena, Montana, Walter Camryn was trained in Russian ballet by Adolph Bolm, Marie Swoboda, Laurent Novikoff, and Muriel Stuart, but has never strayed far from his American roots. A soloist and premier danseur with the various Chicago Opera companies, and with the Page-Stone Ballet and Federal Theatre Ballet throughout the 1930s, Camryn continued to dance for several decades.

However, his first love was teaching; with Bentley Stone, he formed the Stone-Camryn School at 185 West Madison Street, Chicago, in 1940. A year later, Camryn became the artistic director of the Children's Civic Theatre of Chicago and held the post for ten years. It was in this capacity, and with the later Stone-Camryn Ballet, that he demonstrated the strongest characteristic of both his choreography and his teaching: character dancing, with a strong American flavor. His classes have been widely circulated outside the Stone-Camryn School through a pamphlet containing ten beginning classes entitled, *Walter Camryn's Analytical Study of Character Movement and Dances.* His enormous influence on the teaching of character dancing in America has grown with his numerous teachers' courses throughout the United States and Canada.

Walter Camryn is a quiet, powerful person, who is very sure of himself and of his opinions. Although he is a fine teacher of classical ballet, Walter's specialty is character work. This, of course, includes practically everything: minuets, mazurkas, polonaises, square dances, free-style movement, Hungarian rhapsodies, ballroom dances, even yoga. In fact, he conducts classes entirely of yoga, which are his interpretation of what yoga is all about. They are very popular classes.

Walter Camryn has incorporated movements from his character class in his various choreographies. I danced a ballroom dance with him called Valse Cecile, *which he arranged with so much humor and style that it always had to be encored. I adored dancing it with him. His* Reunion, *with music by Chicago's Laura Aborn, was also choreographed with humor and drama for himself, Bentley Stone, and me as participants in a class reunion. Walter specialized in Americana—works such as* Thunder in the Hills, The Shooting of Dan McGrew, *and* Dr. Eli Duffy's Snakeroot *—which crept into his character class. Still, he was able to teach very correctly the dances of many nations.*

Walter was also a most sympathetic performer. I was more than satisfied with him as Don José in my first version of Carmen, *called* Guns and Castanets, *which was set in Civil War Spain. None of us tried to be authentic Spanish, but to give a vivid impression of this very dramatic style. Walter's teaching of Spanish dance in his character class was perhaps his weakest point; he was not naturally volatile in the Iberian manner.*

With Bentley Stone, Walter Camryn was able to build up one of the best ballet schools in the country. Their list of star pupils, from John Kriza to John Neumeier, has been truly remarkable.

CLASSWORK: WALTER CAMRYN, CHICAGO, 1943

Center	Port de Bras
4th pos, R ft pte-tendue front croisé	
Chaîné turns R	
Pas de basque R into arabesque croisé on L ft	L hand on R elbow
Glissade changé R	
Grand jeté onto R ft croisé	
Temps levé on R ft	
Step on L ft, assemblé en tournant L, finish facing front	
Sissonne R, weight on R flat ft, L ft pte-tendue croisé	L arm en haut
Grand rond de jambe en l'air with L leg (front-side-back)	
Renversé	R arm en haut
Come down on L ft, face C1 in 3rd arabesque	
Glissade diag back L	
Double pirouette en dedans on R ft, L leg in attitude devant, lean L	R arm en haut
Finish 5th pos, R ft back	R arm en haut
Lean L, point L ft croisé front	
Repeat to other side	
(Interesting jump)	
R ft pte-tendue back croisé, from C1	R arm diag up R
Glissade diag back L	
1 complete temps levé en tournant on R ft, L leg à la seconde	Arms 5th en haut
Grand jeté diag fwd R on L ft	

Center	Port de Bras
5th pos, R ft front	
Step diag fwd R on R flat ft (temps lié), L ft pte-tendue back	L arm 5th en haut, R arm 2nd
Pivot on L ft (1 turn), putting weight on L ft (come to same place where it was pointed), R ft pte-tendue back croisé	R arm 5th, L arm 2nd
Step back on R ft croisé, balançoire L ft on floor to pte-tendue éffacé (weight on R flat ft)	L arm 5th, R arm 2nd
Plié in 4th pos on L ft, straighten, R ft pte-tendue back éffacé	R arm 5th, L arm 2nd
In this position	
Balançoire (low) with R ft to front croisé	Bring L arm to 5th, R to low 2nd
Double fouetté R, finish R ft back	
Repeat to other side	

Cia Fornaroli Toscanini

CIA FORNAROLI TOSCANINI 1888-1954

Cia Fornaroli, Italy's greatest ballerina of the first half of the twentieth century, was born in Milan. She graduated from the Ballet Academy of the Teatro alla Scala, Milan, where she was a favorite student of Cecchetti.

Fornaroli first came to the United States in 1910 at the invitation of the Metropolitan Opera Ballet to become première danseuse. She remained there four years. Thereafter, she toured America as a member of Anna Pavlova's company and appeared in South America as a guest artist in 1915 and 1920. Upon her return to Italy, Fornaroli became prima ballerina at La Scala and, when Cecchetti died in 1928, was appointed Director of its Ballet Academy. One of her last functions in Italy was ballet mistress of the Venice International Music Festival in 1933. That same year, due to the opposition of Italy's Fascist government to her husband, Dr. Walter Toscanini (son of conductor Arturo), she retired from dancing, resigned all her posts, and left with him for America.

In the late 1930s, Cia Fornaroli taught at the New York studio of Vincenzo Celli (another prize Cecchetti pupil) and, in 1940, was guest teacher for the newly formed Ballet Theatre. Throughout the 1940s, she taught chiefly at her own studio in Carnegie Hall, which is where Ruth Page studied with her. Her classes demonstrated that she was a most loyal disciple of Maestro Cecchetti. Cia Fornaroli retired from teaching, due to poor health, in 1950. Four years later, she died.

A lasting tribute to the memory of Cia Fornaroli as dancer and teacher is the Cia Fornaroli Collection, donated by Dr. Walter Toscanini to the Dance Collection of The New York Public Library at Lincoln Center. Among the treasures collected by Fornaroli and her husband over the years are great milestones in the history of dance instruction, including Enrico Cecchetti's handwritten manual of exercises and technique (St. Petersburg, 1894) and his variations and classroom music.

I was always impressed by the fact that Cia Fornaroli was not only Arturo Toscanini's daughter-in-law, but my old teacher Cecchetti's goddaughter as well. Her classes were very Italian in style, that is, closely related to Cecchetti's method. This was to be expected, as she was a ballerina at La Scala in Milan.

Fornaroli gave the hardest pointe-work class I ever attended; if you could get through this torture, you could get through anything. Most of her pirouettes were from fifth position, which was very hard, but very good for me, as my own fifth position left something to be desired. When her steps really seemed impossible and we were all struggling, Cia would sing, almost fortissimo, "Corragio! Corragio!"

CLASSWORK: CIA FORNAROLI TOSCANINI, NEW YORK, 1946

Center

(Toe—hard)
5th pos, R ft front
Pas de bourrée dessous en tournant
   R (L-R-L)
Relevé on L pte, grand battement rond
   de jambe with R leg (front-side-back)
Relevé on L ft, half turn R, R leg in
   passé, finish 5th pos, R ft front
1 pirouette en dehors R, finish
   5th pos, R ft front
2 pirouettes en dehors R, *without*
   putting R ft down
Pas de bourrée dessous (R-L-R)
Repeat, starting with battement rond
   de jambe, 4 times to same side

5th pos, R ft front
Piqué turn R, stay en pte
Piqué turn L
Close 5th pos, R ft front
Double piqué turn R
Double piqué turn L, coupé on R ft
Piqué on L pte, R ft in front piqué pos
Repeat to R

5th pos, R ft front
Pas de bourrée dessous R (L-R-L),
   finish 5th pos, L ft front
Double pirouette en dehors R
Piqué turn L, R ft in front piqué pos
Piqué turn R
1 fouetté turn R on L ft

Center

Repeat
Relevé on L ft in attitude turns en dehors R
Repeat fouettés and attitude turns
1 fouetté turn R on L ft
Bring R ft sur le cou-de-pied, finish
    5th pos, R ft front
Repeat, same side

(Jump)
5th pos, R ft front
Failli diag fwd R, finish L ft croisé
Step R on R ft and temps levé, L ft
    front croisé
Step R on L ft, grand jeté on R ft,
    L leg en attitude
Assemblé en arrière with L ft
Entrechat-six
Saut de basque diag fwd R, finish on L ft
Step R into temps levé tour en dedans on
    R ft, L leg in passé pos front, stretching
    to arabesque on landing
Jump into saut de basque to L
Repeat to same side

Carmelita Maracci in costume for a dance that demonstrates
her blend of Spanish dancing and classical ballet

CARMELITA MARACCI
B. 1911

From the early 1930s, Carmelita Maracci was acclaimed as a dancer of unique distinction and the creator of a highly nonconformist, intensely personal style. The same terms have been applied to her teaching method —an amalgam of ballet, Spanish, and contemporary dance—which may account for her genuine and devoted, if limited, following in the dance world. With students such as Allegra Kent and Cynthia Gregory to her credit, her distinction as a great teacher is assured.

Maracci was born in Montevideo, Uruguay, of Spanish-Italian parents. She was brought to San Francisco at age two, and California has been her home ever since. Maracci made her local debut in Los Angeles in April 1930, to immediate acclaim. Her concerts consisted primarily of solos and small group works, and her New York appearances, which began in 1937, won critical acclaim.

However, Carmelita Maracci began teaching in 1937, and this has continued to be her principal vocation. Her school, at 1612½ North McCadden, in Hollywood, was never ostentatious, but the training generations of students have received there has been priceless.

Wherever I went on my tours, I always liked to take class with the local teachers of high reputation. One of the most interesting places to go was Los Angeles, where dance developed in isolation from the New York influence that seemed to reach every other part of the nation. The rest of the country was equally unaware of developments in California. I think Lester Horton was the best example of this.

I went to Los Angeles at least once a year from the late 1930s into the early 1940s. Also, my longtime collaborator and costume designer, Nicholas Remisoff, had moved to Palm Springs, and when I wanted him to design the costumes for my Dances With Words and Music, *I had to go there to consult with him. While I was there, I would go the rounds of Los Angeles teachers, including Maria Bekefi, David Lichine, and Eugene Loring. But the one who had always made the greatest impression on me, and still does, was Carmelita Maracci.*

Maracci is a very unusual teacher. Each step that she gave, though rooted in conventional ballet, was done so dramatically and so forcefully that the idea of anything sylphlike flew out the window. In place of ethereality came the beating of toes into the floor, sudden turning in and out of the legs and feet, and the power that one relates more to the modern dance than to the ballet. I loved the strength that one got in the legs, and especially the toes, in her classes. After working with her a while, that same strength carried one easily into the air; her own jumps soared. Carmelita's adagio was often done en pointe with the working leg doing the same movements as if the weight were on the flat foot (nothing is more difficult than that). I wish I could have studied with Carmelita Maracci for a more extended period of time. She really impressed me—hers was ballet with a difference.

These notes on Carmelita's classes are just fragments of combinations that intrigued me or challenged me the most.

CLASSWORK: CARMELITA MARACCI, HOLLYWOOD, 1938

Center	Port de Bras
3rd pos, R ft front	
Turn R knee in, ft just off floor, just crossing L knee	Contract shoulders fwd
Turn R knee out, lower R ft to "5th" pos: L ft pointing straight fwd, R toe crossed over, touching L toe	End arms 4th
Feet together, turned-in 1st pos, facing front	
Weight on L ft	Arms en bas
3 stamps on R demi-pte in 3rd pos	"Rond des mains" [circle hands from wrist] en dehors on 1st stamp
	Arms 5th en haut on 2nd stamp
	"Rond des mains" en dedans on 3rd stamp
Stamp on R ft, sharp small jump fwd, shifting weight from L ft to R ft	Arms sharply to 2nd, then en bas
Repeat to both sides, leaning way back and fluttering hands	
Feet together, face front	
Little jump, pointing R ft to R	

Center	Port de Bras
Slight plié on L ft	Still face front, arms 2nd, elbows turned up
Repeat to L, without coming back to 1st pos	Bring elbows down on jump
Stamps in place, finish L ft pointed front	Arms 4th, R en haut; finish L en haut, look down
Repeat to each side	
("Cuban walk") 3rd pos, R ft front Long step fwd on R ft Bend R knee	Swing L arm fwd waist-high
Step fwd on L ft	Swing R arm fwd waist-high
Swing L hip out-and-in, out-and-in	Arms 5th en haut, look under arms
("High-up walk") 3rd pos, R ft front Go diag fwd R, stepping from one demi-pte to the other, each time bending knee of lifted leg, until ft almost touches hip (legs are turned in)	Arms 5th en haut; lean upper body way back, hold torso while head moves up and down
("Habanera step") 3rd pos, R ft front Lunge to R side on L ft (L profile to public)	Arms 5th en avant, backs of wrists together
Swing R ft over in front of L, doing a kind of two-step Repeat	Flutter R hand just over head
Feet in 1st pos, toes together	Arms 1st Little jerk of shoulders fwd
Deep plié	Arms to 2nd, then 5th en haut at bottom of plié
Straighten knees Repeat	Turn palms to ceiling Arms to 2nd, then 1st L hand on hip Face and look diag fwd L Little jerk of shoulders fwd

Center	**Port de Bras**
Plié	Lift R arm from very low to high overhead Same hand accent
Straighten knees Repeat Repeat first section twice as fast Put weight on R ft, L demi-pte in 3rd pos	Arms low 2nd, "rond des mains," palms facing public and at tension
3rd pos, L ft flat, R demi-pte	"Rond des mains" en dedans near center of body, bring them up 5th en haut, palms facing ceiling
4 stamps on R demi-pte	"Rond des mains" en dehors "Rond des mains" en dedans Repeat hands en dehors and en dedans
Small jump, changing to 3rd pos, R ft flat, L ft demi-pte Repeat to other side	Palms still facing ceiling Arms to 2nd, then 1st
(Alegrias) 3rd pos, R ft front Step R on R flat ft, putting R hip out to R side, stop	Clap hands twice near R side of forehead on stop
Bring L ft up to R ft, L knee turned in Point L ft demi-pte L about one foot from R ft, turn knee out with jerk Repeat 7 times Pose, half-lunge on R ft diag fwd R	Hands in fists, low at sides; look down
Cross L ft over R in front of R ft	

Center	Port de Bras
"Chug" a little, slide R on L ft (All very small on demi-pte, accent the first cross movement each time)	Arms 5th en haut
4 steps R on demi-pte (R-L-R-L), finish L profile to public	R arm up straight and high, L arm low
Repeat "chug" on L ft	
Cross R ft over L in front of L ft	
4 steps back on demi-pte, keeping R ft crossed over in front of L ft	Elbows bent, push away with L hand, then R (pushing hand should be just out from center of waist, other arm should be back)
Repeat 6 times	
4 chaîné turns on demi-pte L	
Finish both feet demi-pte, R profile to public	R arm en haut, L en bas
(My favorite strut step)	
Start facing C1	R arm en haut, L arm en bas, elbow bent
Weight on R ft, L pointed back L éffacé	
Lift L leg up turned in, knee sharply bent	
Stamp L toe-heel diag fwd R, crossed in front of R ft	Sharply turn shoulders L (R shoulder fwd) Look up, snap fingers
Weight on L ft, R pointed diag fwd R, throw hip out to L	Shoulders same; look down, snap fingers
Put R ft in back of L and step on it	Jerk L shoulder fwd; look over L shoulder to L (arms same, snap fingers on after-beat)
Put L ft back to original pos	
Repeat whole step, lifting the feet high and neatly each time	
Repeat a third time	
Lift L ft up, lunge diag fwd R croisé on L ft	Lean way back; raise R arm overhead, L arm low at side
Bring R ft fwd into 3rd pos, demi-plié, hip out to L side	R arm en avant, L arm back, both waist level and elbows bent; look over R arm down at R ft

Center	Port de Bras
Big step back on R ft to lunge pos	
Put L ft in 3rd pos, keeping weight on R ft demi-plié	
Bounce twice to L, making complete turn L and putting L flat ft down twice in 3rd pos (double-time)	L arm en avant, R arm back, both waist level and elbows bent, on first bounce; reverse arms for second bounce
Repeat	
Lift L ft as in beginning	
"Strut" diag fwd R from one demi-pte to the other	Gradually lift arms arrogantly

L*ARRY LONG* B. *1936*

Larry Long was raised in Los Angeles, and it was in California that he started dance lessons with Alexandra Baldina, a Maryinsky ballerina who had danced with Diaghilev's Ballets Russes for the 1909 season, and later settled in America with her husband, Theodore Kosloff. Larry Long's later teachers were the former pupils of Baldina and stars of the Ballet Russe de Monte Carlo, Nana Gollner and Paul Petroff. After four years of study, he joined the Alicia Alonso ballet. In the early 1960s, Long joined the Ruth Page Chicago Opera Ballet, where he created a number of roles in Page ballets and later became ballet master and choreographer. In 1969, Long was invited to join the National Ballet of Washington as ballet master, and subsequently held the same position with the Harkness Ballet of New York.

He returned to Chicago in the early 1970s to co-found the Chicago Ballet with Ruth Page. He also co-founded (in 1971) and directed the Ruth Page Foundation School of Dance. In 1976, Larry Long became director of Ballet International in London, which toured England, Europe, and Africa. He returned to Chicago in 1978 to resume the directorship of the Ruth Page Foundation School, and continues to hold that post.

Larry Long tells me that when he auditioned for me, the only reason I took him into my company was that he did such good "butterflies." Of course, this is not true. But I was glad to find a dancer as fine as Larry who could do a few acrobatic tricks, which I needed for a ballet I was choreographing at the time.

Larry has been with me a long time—over twenty years. He started in the corps de ballet, became a soloist, then ballet master, and is now the director of my school, and can restage any of my ballets, he knows my style so well. Like most American dancers, Larry has studied here, there, and everywhere, but has now developed a teaching style of his own. It is basically very correct ballet, but he dreams up all kinds of fancy combinations. Everyone loves his class, perhaps because he demonstrates so well and shows every step so carefully. He does not yell and scream, but in his quiet way is very forceful. He kept my company well rehearsed, not only technically, but emotionally, and has trained and developed a number of young, potential stars.

Larry Long

CLASSWORK: LARRY LONG, CHICAGO, 1980

Center	Port de Bras
	Port de Bras

Center **Port de Bras**

(Chopin "Mazurka"—3/4 time) (Use character-style arms)
Stand on R ft, L ft pte-tendue back à terre
Balancé L
3 cabrioles R (legs turned in, L arm 5th en haut, R
   clicking heels character-style)   hand on hip
Balancé R
3 cabrioles L (same style as to R) R arm 5th en haut, L
  hand on hip

Step L, sharp développé with R leg R arm 2nd, L hand on hip
   éffacé (C1)
Step R, sharp développé with L leg L arm 2nd, R hand on hip
   éffacé (C2)
Step L, développé (high) with R leg L arm 5th en haut, R arm
   croisé (C2)   in 2nd
Tombé, 4th pos lunge on R ft croisé
Pirouette en dedans R
Close 5th pos, L ft front Arms en bas
Relevé attitude, L leg croisé Arms 2nd
   devant
Close 5th pos, L ft front Arms en bas
Relevé attitude, R leg back croisé Arms 5th en haut
Plié into 4th pos Preparation for pirouette
Multiple pirouettes en dehors R
Finish 4th pos lunge, R leg back, Arms wide 2nd
   straighten
Repeat to other side

*(Tendus and pirouettes to Rachmaninoff's
"Theme of Paganini"—2/4)*
5th pos en face, R ft front
Tendu en croix with R leg (accent out) Arms in opposition to
  working leg
2 battements dégagés with R leg Hold arms in 2nd
   to side (back-front)
Battement dégagé R, finish R leg
   ballonné [passé] pos back
Relevé arabesque, R leg back
Coupé dessous with R ft Arms en bas
Step fwd on L ft to soussus, Arms 2nd
   plié 5th pos, R ft back
3 changements, hold Arms en bas
3 changements, hold

Center	**Port de Bras**
Chassé fwd on L ft, plié 4th pos	Arms 2nd
Double pirouette R, finish 4th pos lunge	
Straighten, R ft pte-tendue back	
Plié 4th pos	
Triple pirouette R, finish 4th pos lunge	
Coupé dessous with R ft	Arms en bas
Step fwd on L ft to soussus	Arms 2nd
Plié 5th pos, L ft front	Arms en bas

(Beats—2/4 time)

5th pos, R ft front	
Changement	Arms en bas
Soubresaut, R ft back	
Entrechat royale	
Soubresaut, L ft back	
Entrechat-quatre	
Soubresaut, L ft back	Arms 2nd
Entrechat-six	Arms move through 1st, 5th en haut, 2nd, to en bas
Soubresaut, R ft back	
Repeat to other side	

(Small jumps to Joplin "Rag")

5th pos, R ft front	Arms en bas
Jeté L	
Jeté R	
Jeté L	
Ballotté to pte-tendue éffacé L	Arms 3rd, opposition
Ballotté to pte-tendue écarté devant R	Arms 2nd
Coupé dessous with R ft	Arms 3rd, opposition
Step on L to C3	Arms to 2nd
Ballonné R leg (turning), finish R leg up in back	Arms high 1st
Glissade back, R leg croisé, through 4th pos	Arms to 2nd
Close 5th pos, L ft front	Arms en bas
Repeat to other side	

(Tchaikovsky "Winter Waltz"—3/4 time)
R ft front croisé, from C3

Center	Port de Bras
Center	**Port de Bras**
Balancé R	Regular arms
Balancé L	
Relevé arabesque turn R on R ft	R arm 5th en haut, L arm 2nd
Close 5th pos, L ft back	Arms en bas
Sissonne R	Arms 2nd
Failli, pas de bourrée L croisé (L-R-L) to C1	Arms high 1st
Chassé R, pas de bourrée R to C1	Arms 2nd
Step on L ft, grand jeté on R ft	Arms 2nd arabesque
Step on L ft across to C1	
Posé into arabesque on R ft	Arms 1st arabesque
Chassé back on L ft	Arms 2nd
Balancé L (turning under)	Arms high 1st
Step on R ft, cabriole back	Arms 3rd arabesque
Chassé L, pas de bourrée L (R-L-R)	Arms 2nd
Grand jeté on L ft, failli R ft over	Arms 2nd arabesque, R arm fwd
Pas de basque, finish C1	
Step into balancé and repeat to other side	

Modern Dance

MODERN DANCE is perhaps

an old-fashioned term by now, but I suppose that everything that is not ballet, ethnic, jazz, or social dance could still be called "modern."

I never studied with Martha Graham or Doris Humphrey, although I admired them tremendously, because I did not want to be influenced by them. I only went out of sheer curiosity to a few of Mary Wigman's classes in Dresden and Berlin. While some balletomanes used to say, "Modern dance is just bad ballet," I disagreed completely. I found that the classes of Wigman had a lot to offer.

However, I never gave up ballet for modern dance, even when I became Harald Kreutzberg's partner. I almost always took a ballet class before I took his inspirational, nonpedantic, hour-and-a-half modern exercises. Another close association with modern dance came when the quartet from the José Limón Company appeared with my company, Les Ballets Américains, in Paris in 1950, dancing The Moor's Pavane and La Malinche. Limón, Pauline Koner, Betty Jones, and Lucas Hoving also danced in my ballets on those programs.

My ballets have always been in a very free style; I think that many of them cannot be called ballet or modern. Fortunately, for choreographers today, a mixture of styles is very much de rigeur and dancers must be acquainted with both ballet and modern in order to perform.

Mary Wigman, ca. 1930

MARY WIGMAN 1886-1973

Mary Wigman is the artist most closely identified with the European modern dance known as "Expressionist" dance. She was born in Hanover, Germany, and moved toward the arts, first as a student of music and literature. She was greatly impressed by a performance of students of Eurythmics, the physical movement approach to the study of musical rhythm founded by Emile Jaques-Dalcroze, and, in 1911, enrolled in the Dalcroze school in Dresden-Hellerau.

Finding the Dalcroze system too limited for her needs, Wigman went to Switzerland two years later to enroll in a course taught by Rudolf von Laban, dance theorist and champion of dance for its own sake. Wigman responded more completely to Laban's method, even becoming his assistant, and remained at the school until 1919. But she had started working on her own as early as 1914, when she gave her first solo performance, which was not successful.

In those years, Wigman began to explore the expressive possibilities of dance as a reaction to the sterile formality of the classical ballet. A spontaneous evocation of the full range of human emotion and passion was the goal of her movement, and even her early dances reflected the profundity of those emotions.

In 1920, Wigman opened a school in Dresden, the Mary Wigman Zentralschule. It was a training center for dancers, teachers, and choreographers who wished to explore the potential of the "New German Dance" —"making visible what one feels." Classes began at 9 A.M. and continued until noon. In addition to the group classes, a Wigman professional student was expected to take an afternoon private lesson.

Shortly after her school opened, Wigman formed a dance group, which made two triumphant United States tours in 1931 and 1932. Her leading pupil and assistant, Hanya Holm, remained in America and opened a Wigman school in New York. Its announced goals were:

To transform the uneloquent body into an expressive instrument.

To build this instrument so that it can be played upon by inner command or outer design.

To encourage individual style.

To teach a universal language of dance.

To prepare students for stage, concert or group dancing.

Holm soon developed her own style of teaching and choreographing, as did many other outstanding Wigman pupils, including Gret Palucca, Yvonne Georgi, Kurt Jooss, and Harald Kreutzberg. However, Wigman's goals were not betrayed—her pupils were not committed to perpetuating any one style of movement, but were liberated individuals who developed their own distinctive forms of self-expression in dance.

I was in Berlin with my mother in 1930, when, out of curiosity, I went to Mary Wigman's advanced class. Mother, who had never had a dancing lesson in her life, took a beginners' class. We also studied with Wigman in Dresden as well as with one of her principal teachers, Lies Fox, in Munich. Mother was so impressed that she invited Lies Fox to come to Indianapolis to teach her friends. As far as I was concerned, Mother's friends were "old" ladies (not one probably older than fifty) and, like Mother, they liked these simple exercises. Our black cook was invited to watch a class; when Mother asked her what she thought of it, her reply was, "Well, that ain't nothin' but bumps, and grinds, and messin' around!" It is true that the hips and pelvic region, unlike ballet, were very important. However, what impressed me most was Wigman's use of Anspannung *and* Abspannung *(tension and relaxation), sudden shifts in body weight, and repetition of steps or movements mounting into physical crescendos. These seemed to be really new in dance.*

Most of Wigman's exercises were quite simple, but the expressivity required and even the frequent awkwardness of the movements were what made them interesting. Running, walking, skipping, falling, and sudden stops were done with the utmost feeling. For me, the classes were fun because they seemed so relaxed and informally enjoyable after all the set, difficult exercises of classical ballet. I would say that Wigman's classes were marvelous for actors, just as Dalcroze classes were good for musicians. Both were splendid for amateurs of all kinds, and even professional dancers could benefit from a return to the source of basic movement, from which to develop more ease and natural expression.

MARY WIGMAN TECHNIQUE

I find the words *Anspannung* and *Abspannung* very expressive (much more so than *tension* and *relaxation*)

1. On half-toe in 2nd pos, knees   Arms in high 2nd, fingers
   very straight, head back   stretched

ANSPANNUNG

2. Feet flat in small 2nd pos, body   Arms droop to floor
   bending fwd, all parts of body
   completely relaxed

ABSPANNUNG

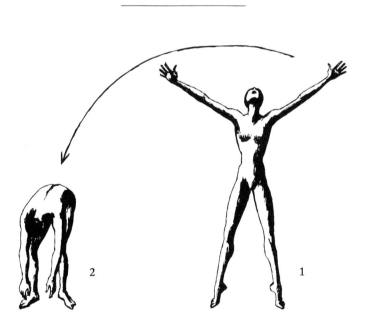

2   1

1. Face C1
   Balancé R, R ft flat, L half-toe
     in back, about a foot apart
   Upper body and head turned R

   Both arms low: R arm
     straight back low; L
     elbow bent, hand to R
     side of body

2. Balancé to L, reversing pos

3. Reverse pos to R

4.

   Lift arms overhead to 5th
     en haut (very free style)

5. Stay on R ft flat, L ft pointed L,
     slightly front
   With body still facing C1, bend L

   Arms in 3rd, R arm up

1. Temps levé on L ft, knee bent, R leg
    straight front (facing C1)
    Bend fwd until head almost touches
    R leg

    Arms straight and
       stretched beyond R ft,
       hands almost touching,
       palms down

2. Temps levé on R ft, L kicked back
    and bent up to ceiling

    R arm in 5th en haut, L
       arm in 2nd (freely),
       head tossed up and
       back

CLASSWORK: MARY WIGMAN, DRESDEN, 1930

[*Terms*]

Abspannung: A (relaxation)

Anspannung: S (tension)

Hips, arms, and steps move in figure eights.

Run very fast (leaning slightly fwd) on half-toe; same movement, feet close together as though really on toes. Very effective.

Just walk in patterns. Effective.

One person in each corner. From opposite corners, two run to center and leap past each other; two remaining run to center and leap. Keep it up and it is very effective.

Big class, lines of six. Very primitive simple rhythms and steps like African war dance. Start with small steps and crescendo.

Totenmal [see illustration]. Death figures run about (effective only when they run fwd a few steps, then sway back a few steps) over platform, all fall. Girl comes in with cross; runs fwd very hard and stops in S pose; runs again; sways back a little (back to audience) onto R ft, L half-toe; falls suddenly onto L knee; puts cross on platform and girls take it; falls onto floor. One girl trembles and falls down with knees bent under like Doris [Humphrey].

Totenmal

Elizabeth (Wigman's sister). Lie down on floor; get up gradually; pose S in sitting pos; slowly to knee and pose; slowly get up and pose. Repeat gradually going down. Repeat entirely A, as if in a dream. Get up and dance a little as though you are on a cloud; gradually sink down again. Repeat entirely S.

Start a movement very small and gradually open up to very wide movements; do this exercise S and A.

Stand quietly, one ft in front of the other; take a deep breath and put weight onto front ft, everything A; let breath out and put weight on back ft. Do this several times, then with one step front and one back; two front and two back; add one step each time through five, always with same feeling.

Draw a letter (any letter) in air, first small, then with very big movements; walk or run the same letter on floor.

Run around bent slightly fwd as though something were drawing (pulling) you; run around as though something were pulling you, but you do not want to go. Shut your eyes, put hand on someone's shoulder, and let that person lead you around.

Dance subjects for improvisation. Escape: you have been in a shipwreck and wake up on a desert island, you look around, wonder where you are, etc. Magician: draw a magic circle, get in, do a dance like a magician.

Hands (fingers) open; use fingers like scratching. Effective.

Go fwd, step and kick loosely; do same going backward.

Go backward in figure eight.

Kneel on both knees. Lean straight back (no backbend); put hands on floor in back; keeping body in same pos, take hands off floor and put arms in front.

Sit on floor, knees up, L arm resting relaxed on L knee. Put R hand on floor in back; put R ft out on floor, body up off floor S; come back to starting pos.

BERLIN, 1930

Lie on floor; have someone hold your feet. Move shoulders, turning first to L, then to R quickly (move whole bust).

Lie on floor. Lift body like backbend, but parallel to floor; lift L leg up high and R hand up from floor.

Lie on floor. Lift only bust up; stiffen neck; only have head touching.

Always start lesson walking fast-slow on half-toe and down; go into run.

Leap (with run). Leap with head and arms bent fwd; run; leap looking back as though trying to kick head.

Lie on floor on stomach. Raise upper body, leaving stomach on floor; bend way back; bend knees, leaving knees on floor, and try to touch head with toes.

Two people together (A and B) face each other. A steps on R ft quickly; immediately puts weight onto L ft back croisé; temps levé immediately on L ft. B does same, only putting L ft front. A steps on R ft again quickly (like a grace note); crosses L ft over in front and relevé immediately (accented). Continue going down center.

Side to side movement. Step on R ft; L ft half-toe to side on floor; bend way over to R side (two counts). Bring L ft up to R; bend to L side. Do it all very A.

Walk three steps straight fwd: first step on R ft, swing both arms around to R (only moving from waist); second step on L ft, swing to L; on third step, swing to R and hold S pose (turning fully back for three counts). Continue. Repeat, only with arms crossed in front and moving only from waist up.

Toe exercises. Put ft down on ball and heel; lift toes up and down. Do same exercises with toes as with fingers. Stand in 1st pos and wiggle toes, moving ft fwd without lifting heel and sole.

Skip, turning very fast; make wheel; fall. Skip in place, turning, and fall.

Walk, stepping on half-toe and lifting shoulders very high each time.

Put R hip out to R (R ft turned out); walk to R, crossing L ft always over in front of R. As hip goes out, let impetus throw R arm up naturally.

Walk, slowly lifting arm; stop when it is highest; stay quite still (very dramatic effect). Repeat, one person leading and three side-by-side following, copying leader's movements.

Step-kick en tournant, everything A; throw arms out (can be made very funny).

Make big circle. One girl goes to center; step-kicks very fast, shaking all over very A; everyone in circle stamps feet and claps hands; end everyone shaking and kicking. Looks very primitive.

S on half-toe, arms up. Take falling steps fwd, each one getting lower and lower, until you finally sink to ground. Do it only one step up and one down (while standing on R ft, L ft is pointed straight back, *not* to side).

Profile to audience, stand on L ft, R ft pointed to side. Turn toe slightly in, way out, put heel down; do half turn, ending with weight on R ft; step onto L ft, swinging hip out to L at same time; put weight onto R ft, swinging hip to R. Repeat to other side. Repeat with full turn.

Arms crossed on chest, go diag fwd L, facing front R corner (C1): step on L ft half-toe, lifting R leg and *hip*; come down on R ft in front of L; quick step on L ft; suddenly put R hip out to R. From this pos, repeat.

Lean fwd just as far as you can without falling; suddenly let your body fall fwd very A; lean back as far as possible without falling; suddenly lean fwd very A. Do it first with steps in between, then without steps. (Latter is difficult, but good for diaphragm.)

Upper back stretch. Put both hands around bottom of ft; stretch leg out straight in front; lean way over front as far as possible.

Run five counts; do rotary movement, starting with hips and continuing like a spiral through upper body.

Walk five steps diag fwd R, criss-cross; swing hips around from R to L; throw upper body clear around to L in same pos (all A). Facing ready to go L, repeat in zigzag.

Do rond de jambe off floor, lifting hip way up each time and well turned out.

CLASSWORK: MARY WIGMAN TECHNIQUE, LIES FOX, MÜNCHEN, 1930

Do S and A with hands: first S way up, both arms high, fingers and chest and everything completely stiff, *suddenly* A and fall from waist. Do same, S up and A backward. Same, S sideward and fall to side. Do both sides, then S up and A down; leave body in A; go all the way around, bending always loosely from waist. Repeat in 2nd pos.

Important. Jump temps levé on L ft, R leg up in attitude straight back; come down to squat, L knee up and out, R knee flat on floor, body and head way down and A; fall to R, or get up without changing squat pos; do jump again.

Good for ballet. Put R toe in front; come down on R ft very softly, L half-toe on floor in back; bounce up and down in this pos; bounce whole body A. Do it slowly, then fast: three times with body down, three times with body and head back.

Swing leg front (bent), then back, all A. Do it jumping, only without lifting ft clear off ground.

Stamp hard on R ft, S; hold three counts; walk on half-toe very A, three counts.

Three short quick breaths in and out.

Run; stop suddenly in S and suddenly A; turn; take definite pose; run again; S and A. Effective.

Walk quietly. Step on R ft turned out; rise on both feet half-toe; without coming down, put L half-toe in front; come down on R (back) ft. Repeat, only when you get on half-toe, make half turn; come down; finish; and start again.

2nd pos. Bend to all sides, first S, then A.

Start plié in 1st pos (stomach down [in]). Rise to half-toe slowly; get faster and continue jumping (like ballet), S while in air (knees stiff).

INDIANAPOLIS, 1930

Swing arms in front A; then S in any pos and walk that way; run and pose in S and A, in same number of counts. Repeat.

Good for legs & back. Lie on floor, R knee up, R ft on floor, L leg up to knee turned in flat on floor; rise part-way up; shift to other side without wiggling.

Effective ending. Feet in 2nd pos turned in, knees bent way in front. Gradually sink to floor, staying in sort of backbend pos; bring feet together in back (ordinary kneeling pos); put head back.

2nd pos, knees bent. Bend to R, arms A, L arm lying on head, R arm near waist (4th pos); repeat to L. Repeat without stopping in between.

Gymnastic. Lie on floor on stomach. Rise on arms (hands on floor, elbows stiff), toes touching floor (knees straight); reach R hand up; turn over, facing ceiling, still supported on arms; lift other hand over. Continue so in circle, do not change pos of body.

Whole class walks around in circle; each person walks in little individual circle.

Legs. On three counts: in 4th pos, plié R ft in front, L ft on floor in back (L knee straight); shift weight to L ft and plié, R leg straight; plié on R ft again. On count 4, straighten R and L knees, point L toe in back; bring L ft fwd. Repeat, L ft in front.

Stand on half-toe (feet apart, R ft in front), both arms up diag front R, head back. Swing arms down and up to L, at same time doing plié, all with very strong sweeping movement.

Développé R leg front, like kick, rising on L half-toe; come down in lunge pos; step on L ft. Repeat to same side. All body and arms open wide up, very S.

Good exercise. 1st pos. Rise on half-toe, at same time swinging both arms up overhead, then down.

Lift arms overhead straight; lift first one shoulder, then the other. Repeat very fast. Repeat, rising on one half-toe (other heel on floor), then on other.

Swing back (like preparing for leap); run fwd fast; stop suddenly and hold any S pose without moving. Difficult.

Step sideward on L ft; bend to L very A with arms dangling down; bring R ft up to L; bend way over to R. Continue going sideward.

Go fwd, almost kneeling on L ft, R ft turned out strongly on floor, arms out to sides; bounce up and down on R ft, hitting floor with L knee each time. Continue going fwd.

2nd pos plié (bounce); bend way over to R, touching R hand to floor; same to L. Keep bouncing up and down with plié each time. Repeat with upper body and arms A.

Go fwd on R ft, almost kneeling on L; rise on R half-toe, L leg trying to kick back of head, both arms up overhead.

Start as though doing regular leap onto R ft, but hit R ft against L knee (just above knee); kick L ft to head in back. Repeat, only pause on L half-toe, R ft on L knee; pose that way.

Exercise for softness of legs. Plié on R ft to side (like lunge); straighten knee, bringing L ft up to R; do regular waltz movement. Repeat to other side: start same way; after lunge, immediately take three steps on half-toe.

Exercise for stomach and hips. Swing R hip to side, then up to L, and down (complete circle). Do it with real swing, everything circular.

Difficult but very good. Feet in 2nd pos, pelvis up. Bend back without much backbend; touch L heel with R hand, then R heel with L hand. Do it very fast.

Feet in 2nd pos, pelvis up. Touch R hand to R heel, then L hand to L heel, without much backbend.

Important for poise. Take deep breath, rising on half-toe, everything up and S; sink down straight (like accordian closes) without fwd or sideward bend. Do it very slowly.

Tread. Shift weight from one ft to the other on whole ft in groups of eight counts: move fwd, at same time bending front, side, back, side, front (complete circle). Repeat, turning.

Harald Kreutzberg

HARALD KREUTZBERG
1902 - 1968

Born in Reichenberg, Czechoslovakia, Harald Kreutzberg became the greatest male exponent of the German modern, or Expressionist, dance and its most original. He studied briefly with Mary Wigman in Leipzig and Dresden, but it is most probable that his training there was simply a formality. As opposed to Wigman's somber nature, Kreutzberg's was elfin, yet spiritual.

His unique stage persona was discovered quite early and won him an engagement as a soloist with the Hanover Opera in 1922. Two years later, he joined the Berlin Staatsoper, where he created the role of the Fool in choreographer Max Terpis' 1926 *Don Morte*. This is the role for which he shaved his head and never again appeared otherwise. Kreutzberg came to the attention of the theatrical genius, Max Reinhardt, and acquired an international reputation by appearing in three successive Reinhardt productions: *The Miracle, A Midsummer Night's Dream,* and *Jedermann.* The following year, 1928, he formed a partnership with the dancer, Yvonne Georgi. They and his lifelong accompanist, Friedrich Wilckens, toured the United States and Europe to great acclaim.

Kreutzberg first danced with Ruth Page in 1933 and performed with her in Japan in 1934 and throughout the United States until 1936. In addition to his duet concerts with Georgi and Page, Kreutzberg made many solo concert tours (1937, 1947, 1948, and 1953 in America), performing such outstanding dances from his repertoire as *Three Mad Figures* and *Angel of the Annunciation.* His last stage appearance was with the Chicago Lyric Opera as Death in Ruth Page's 1965 production of *Carmina Burana.*

Kreutzberg was above all a performing artist but, as revealed by Ruth Page's extensive notes, he did teach classes in his own style. In 1955, close to the end of his performing career, Kreutzberg opened a school in Bern, Switzerland, where he taught in the last years of his life.

Harald Kreutzberg was brilliant and successful his whole life, although he almost never practiced. Except for a few months in Mary Wigman's "dilettante" class, and a little work with Gret Palucca and Yvonne Georgi (who toured with him as partner), his only teacher was the Lord in Heaven.

When he appeared in Don Morte, *he met for the first time its composer, Friedrich Wilckens, who was to become his longtime pianist and companion. After this production, his baldness became a trademark that lent him distinction. It was Max Reinhardt who discovered his genius and allowed him to reveal it in the role of the Master of Ceremonies in Gozzi's* Turandot *in Salzburg.*

Kreutzberg's classes were something very special and unique. It was only a short course, without system or construction to build up a dancer progressively. He really did not teach at all, but improvised whole series of dancelike exercises, accompanied by Wilckens. The members of the class just followed along. As Kreutzberg was one of the greatest dancers in the world, he was a real inspiration to his pupils. His so-called teaching was as fascinating as his dancing, without any real control of his extraordinary body. When he jumped (not high at all), his natural attitude was so excellent that one thought he was standing still in the air. There still exists a Kreutzberg Academy in Bern, Switzerland.

I became Kreutzberg's partner in 1933 and toured with him all over the United States and in Japan. We choreographed our duets together and, for him, everything seemed so easy. He truly led a charmed life. My association with him and Wilckens was most felicitous, providing some of the happiest moments in my life.

KREUTZBERG TECHNIQUE

1. Stand in big 2nd pos, knees straight

   Body en face, head facing C6, slightly back, R profile to public

   R elbow bent, R hand (fingers stretched) on R breast; L arm in 2nd, palm facing ceiling

2. L half-toe, L knee in plié; R leg front attitude (turned in, toes up)

   Body facing C6, R profile to public

   R arm straight out from shoulder in 2nd, palm facing public

   L elbow bent near R upper leg, lower arm straight up, palm to public

3. Step R
   Lunge L flat
   Body facing C6, R profile to public

   Both elbows bent close
      to body, lower arms
      straight to C6, palms
      facing each other

4. Rise on toes close together in 1st pos

   Arms 5th en haut (elbows
      almost straight), backs
      of hands to public

5. Plié
   Jump up, knees very bent and turned
      out, feet close together, toes pointed
   Body facing C1

   Arms straight out from
      shoulder, lower arms
      near each side of body,
      hands in fists near each
      side of waist

1. R half-toe, knee straight
   L leg front, about 2 feet off
      floor, knee straight
   Body facing C1, head facing public (C5)

   Elbows bent, hands
      clasped under chin

2. Weight on L ft front croisé, R ft pointed
      back croisé
   Body facing C5, bent slightly fwd

   Hands clasped near upper
      legs, thumbs up; eyes
      look up R

3. L half-toe, knee bent
   R leg up in front attitude, toes up
   Body facing C6, head facing public,
      but eyes up L

   L arm straight front from
      shoulder, L hand
      (fingers stretched)
      crossing over R ankle
      to outside of R ft
   R arm overhead, elbow
      bent and brought
      across to L of face,
      index and little finger
      straight, middle fingers
      bent down

4. Jump, feet together, toes pointed,
      legs straight, knees together,
      torso bent R
   Body en face, eyes up R

   R arm in 2nd, lower arm
      straight up, palm to
      public; L elbow bent
      shoulder high, L hand
      touching L side of body

1   2   3   4

5. Legs very wide 2nd pos, knees straight,
       back to public
   Bend fwd, head between legs

   Bring arms through legs,
       upper arms shoulder
       high, elbows bent,
       hands (fingers
       stretched) one on each
       side of hips

6. Feet 1st, turned out, toes off floor,
       legs straight
   Body en face, head facing C6

   Arms in 1st, hands
       touching body, one on
       each side of upper leg,
       backs of hands to
       public (C6)

1. Temps levé on R ft, leg straight
   L knee bent and turned out, L ft
      (flexed) near inside front of upper
      R thigh, toes up
   Body en face, head looking L

   L arm straight in low 2nd,
      back of hand just above
      L knee, palm facing
      ceiling; R elbow bent,
      R hand over top of
      head, back of hand
      almost resting on L
      side of forehead

2. Plié, L ft near R in "loose" 1st pos
   Jump, both knees very bent and high,
      feet in kind of 5th pos, almost touching
      underneath of thighs
   Torso and head lean L, R profile to public

   Arms 3rd (L front, wrist
      near R breast); R
      elbow up

3. Kneel on L leg, sitting on L heel, half-toe;
   R leg in high 2nd pos en l'air
   Body en face, head slightly R

   R arm in 2nd, hand
      touching R ft; L elbow
      bent shoulder-high,
      lower arm down, back
      of hand to public

Succession of movement

Body facing C6

A) Lunge L, look R

L elbow bent and reaching overhead, clasping R side of face; R elbow bent, lower arm up, hand on L side of face

B) Legs same pos

R elbow bent, R hand on R side of face (4th and 5th fingers bent in to palm); L elbow bent, lower arm up, wrist bent with hand "drooping," palm to floor

C) In lunge pos, contract stomach, shoulders hunched fwd

Arms straight out front of body, just below shoulder-high, hands clasped together

A   B   C

CLASSWORK: HARALD KREUTZBERG, SALZBURG, 1932

[*A* is relaxation; *S* is tension]

Step on L ft and plié, lifting R ft up, knee bent; arms S straight down, shoulders high; put R ft fwd on floor, toes up. Repeat to other side, going fwd.

S step. Weight on R half-toe, L ft down on floor; both arms down straight (fists). Gradually plié on R ft, keeping body S all the time. Repeat to other side. Repeat, turning body around L when you go R, and R when you go L. Repeat, A as you turn.

Step onto L ft with big plié, R leg straight out to R side; R shoulder raised and R arm sliding down R leg. Do it first S, then lightly get up; take big step R and draw L ft up to R; swing arms R. Then do it jumping (heavy, almost like peasant).

Stand on one ft, hip thrown out to side; do stomach rotation (difficult to balance).

Throw R hip to R (standing on R ft); lift L leg straight L; bend over sideward toward L leg.

Jump fwd into 2nd pos plié, stomach fwd; bend back; straighten knees; bend fwd touching floor.

Step R, R hip out. Through force of outward movement, let R arm come up R; lean over and touch floor.

Big 2nd pos. Plié on R ft; R arm stiff and straight out R without moving; L arm straight out L, bring it over to R, clap R hand with L, bring across chest to straight out L. Repeat S, then A.

Go straight fwd: weight on L ft, R ft fwd; step on L ft, then R. Start softly, then gradually make each movement stronger until on count 8, fall fwd on the floor.

2nd pos. Go from one half-toe to other, slowly, then faster and faster, with jumps.

Plié fwd onto R ft, L ft pointed in back; straighten R and L knees, gradually raising whole body, both arms straight out to side, head back. Whole thing very S.

Facing audience, hop fwd in arabesque, arm and leg long and very stretched out.

Go diag fwd R: step on L flat ft; lift R knee high; bend back. Sharp movements.

Go diag fwd R: rise on L half-toe; kick R leg diag fwd R; bend way back; fall way fwd on R ft (big lunge); continue, slapping R hand on floor, then L (six counts, each one very definite).

Go diag fwd: temps levé jump on L ft, L knee straight; kick R leg up in air, leg very straight. Repeat with leg straight, passé, straight.

Plié on R ft fwd, 4th pos, L ft pointed back. As you go through, putting weight on front ft, bring R shoulder fwd, R arm following through and lifting shoulder-high in front. Turn back to public; plié on L ft (which is now fwd); repeat movement with L shoulder, bringing L arm fwd. Stay with back to public; plié, putting weight back on R ft; bring L shoulder and arm back. Stay with back to public; plié fwd on R ft; bring R arm fwd.

Slow movements (each one eight counts). Slide to R on R ft; lift R arm (movement from hip) and stretch it out to R; turn to face L; plié, bringing weight onto L ft; bring R shoulder through and R arm straight to L. Stay facing L; plié on R ft (which is in back), L ft pointed in front; let both arms come down near body (almost like révérence); turn to face R; lift shoulders and whole body up, both arms at sides (slightly in front); kneel on R knee in eight counts. All must be very slow and flowing.

Go diag fwd R: two lunges; little fast running steps, stopping on both feet half-toe, both arms overhead (*do not* relax); let arms and upper body continue to move fwd (feet as though glued to floor); hold as long as you can; fall. Repeat, only when you stop on half-toe, instead of falling, half turn upper body so that you face diag back, and run heavily (almost lunges) back to where you started. Repeat, only stopping on R half-toe with L leg up in front and then fall fwd.

Walk fwd as though reaching out fwd for something; both arms overhead, but reaching fwd as far as possible; legs very stiff. Do sort of rond de jambe on floor with R ft; step fwd onto R ft; do same with L ft. All half-toe, or only come down on heel as you step fwd in front; knees always very stiff.

Go fwd: rise on L half-toe; drag R toe pointed on ground in kind of rond de jambe en dedans (bring R shoulder up and around); end with plié on R ft in front.

Go fwd fast: arms straight out to sides; cross one ft in front of the other (use hips) like jazz step. Lift L ft from floor each time. Repeat, with feet on floor, staying on half-toe all the time.

Step fwd on R ft, arms very stiff; back on L ft; fwd on R ft again. Continue walking fwd this way. Each time you go fwd, cross arms (very stiff and stretched out as long as possible), elbows crossed and touching; on back step, open arms stiffly to sides. Repeat, with double-time movement as you cross arms.

Lean over fwd in 2nd pos; swing R-L-R, very A, then suddenly rise, very S. Temps levé; hold; look sharply down L. Temps levé again; look up; temps levé again; look down R.

Jump, feet in 2nd pos; suddenly shoot R arm over L (as though lunging with arm); very calmly and A, walk four steps R, gradually lifting R arm up; suddenly go into the accented lunge again. Repeat whole exercise very A.

Feet together, go fwd with little jump. Arms down and very S (fists). As you do little jump, lift shoulders, arch back, and go fwd with little jerk (like gypsy).

Jump (small) in 2nd pos; turn R, elbows bent and fists clenched (look to R). Then little jumps in place (three fast); turn body very quickly R-L-R sharply; repeat the first bigger and accented.

Eight turns on half-toe with both arms straight out to side. Eight turns on half-toe with R arm near L side, L arm in back near R side, elbows bent sharply.

Two slow steps R; two quick steps R; rise on both feet half-toe, with sudden quick movement.

Run fwd with big heavy lunge steps, each time raising arms a little higher; end on half-toe with both arms overhead; gradually relax and fall fwd. Repeat without relaxing, as though your feet were glued to the floor, but your upper body tries to go on.

Feet 2nd pos; hop from one to the other. First, throw R arm up diag fwd R, then L arm up diag fwd L; R down R, then L down L. Start very easily, gradually get wilder and wilder, throw arms as though you wanted to throw them away.

Lunge jump four times R (heavy), four times L; hop four times on R half-toe, very delicately, four on L half-toe.

Step diag fwd L on R ft, lifting R shoulder; take three more steps (L-R-L) very, very low (almost kneeling); go R, taking four steps very high, arms very soft.

Jump on L ft, kicking R leg straight out R; come down on R ft; pas de bourrée en tournant en dehors L; jump high, keeping both knees straight.

Lunge fwd on R ft (quietly); lean fwd as far as possible, L leg straight, R leg plié; straighten, everything S, both arms straight back near hips, chin as far fwd as possible. Repeat, pushing both arms fwd instead of back. Repeat, jumping into the lunge. Repeat, lifting back ft up into arabesque. Then start, standing on R ft, L knee bent; slowly stretch L leg out in back; both arms stretch fwd till everything is S; leap into arabesque.

CHICAGO, 1933

Excellent for back. Hold R arm out R; hold without moving it; turn R under arm; turn all the way around. Repeat to other side.

Walk backward: L arm up high, bend way back; R arm up high, bend way back; both arms up high, bend way back.

Good for big stretch. Walk backward: start leaning way over in front, both hands on floor; walk backward, lifting arms up overhead; come fwd on count 1 again.

Waltz movement. Waltz fwd (diag line), almost touching floor in front; waltz backward, opening arms wide at sides and bending way back. Big sweeping movement.

Walk backward, but reach ft and leg way out (back) each time.

Put R hip way out R; fall R as far as possible, until you put L ft over croisé as far as possible; step on R ft again, R hip out to side; bring L ft up to R. Repeat to other side, letting yourself go as much as possible. Repeat with arms leading to both sides.

Body wave. Bend knees; put hips fwd; bend back, then up. Do slowly, then fast with steps.

Lunge fwd four times (almost running); turn suddenly to side and run away very lightly.

LOS ANGELES, 1933

Walk on half-toe, arms stretched up and legs stretched, everything up; suddenly walk with deep plié, everything as small as possible, arms around knees. Very effective.

Walk backward from arabesque on R ft: step back on L ft, R ft pointed in front; draw both hands from knees over body, go clear up, stretch arms up high overhead, bend way back.

Walk fwd in 2nd pos: head down, both arms bent fwd; step from side to side, body bent fwd (back parallel to ceiling) and swaying (do not bend) from side to side with each step.

Flop over L, putting weight on L ft, dragging R ft along floor (everything A); step R on R ft (hip out); put L ft in back of R ft; bring L ft up close to R ft; step on L half-toe, lift R ft off floor; lift R hip up, at same time come down on R ft. Repeat to same side. Repeat with jumping, S and A. Repeat little and fast.

CHICAGO, 1934

Step on R ft plié, arms and body down; step back L-R-L in place, lifting shoulders up and back. Do this very A, then S.

Go fwd: jump twice heavily in 1st pos, bending way over R, everything relaxed; repeat, bending L. Repeat, bringing R hand and arm near body around in front (about waist-high); swing it out-in to R side and back, twisting upper body way around R and back. Repeat, almost kneeling on R knee, doing same upper twist with upper body. Repeat, going into arabesque on R ft, stretching out as far as possible. Repeat, doing different kinds of turns (e.g., both feet flat on floor, half-toe): start turns on half-toe, everything very straight and S, arms straight out to side; turn without turning head; turn with feet in same way, but bending upper body way back.

Run three counts R starting with R ft (two runs to each count, R-L); on count 4, hop on R ft; turn suddenly; start running L. Repeat, running heavily with lunges. Repeat, running in big semicircles, low and high.

Back to public, step backward on R ft (small step with slight plié), bending upper body back, raising arms to sides, up overhead, down together in front; bring L ft up to R ft in 1st pos (not turned out), lifting arms up as preparation before starting again.

Jumps. Go diag fwd L: plié on L ft; pas de chat fwd; run fwd R-L-R quickly; end with big accent on R ft (like lunge, forceful). Repeat, but after last lunge, small jumps quickly back (L-R), as though R ft from lunge could not stay on floor. Repeat.

Balance steps. Stand on one ft; lift other leg up, knee bent; bend head over to touch ft; straighten and slowly down.

Music crescendos—start with slow steps and increase tempo. 2nd pos. Swing both arms soft and low R, then down and L; bend back (L profile to public), both arms back overhead; lift R ft off floor; step onto R ft, swinging both arms over R. Repeat to other side.

On half-toe, stretch both arms way up; keep one arm S and the other A, letting it fall down to side.

Run, starting slowly; continuing with crescendo, turn on half-toe; pause; continue the run backward. Do movement as though floating.

Sit on floor, both legs out in front. Cross R leg over L leg; lean way back, lifting legs off floor; change legs in air, crossing L over R, at same time pulling yourself up and fwd. Repeat, going back as far as possible.

2nd pos, knees straight. Bend down, touching floor, upper body A; lift up and take deep breath, stretching as high as possible in eight counts; let breath out suddenly and drop body to floor again. Repeat, up in two movements and two breaths; down, letting breath out in two movements. Repeat four times. Repeat, lifting one leg up with breath; bring it down to floor and let breath out as you bend back (slightly sideward). Repeat four times. Repeat to other side.

R ft lifted up in back, R arm up in back. Take two steps backward (R-L); rise on both feet half-toe, at same time lifting L arm from down through big semicircle front, end overhead; immediately in one movement, go down on both knees (feet always in same place) from half-toe; go fwd onto knees,

at same time leaning back and landing on bent R elbow on floor; raise to
L knee, lifting R arm back through overhead to diag fwd L, at same time
putting R ft around in front of L leg; get up turning; finish in starting pos.
Repeat, doing last movement to knees slowly in eight counts.

1st pos, knees straight. Jump three times; A and fall, kneeling on R knee, R
instep flat on floor, L ft flat on floor, L knee up, arms and head A and
leaning over in front; lie down and get up quickly. Repeat.

Step fwd on one ft, then on the other slightly sideward, very A for eight
counts; suddenly run two big steps and a lot of small steps R, falling against
R wall; run to L wall; run to R wall.

Three hops (big, clear to other side of room) R on R ft, L leg up in 2nd: on
first hop, make big movement with R arm, palm out in front (big circle
from L over to R); on second hop, bring R arm in, elbow bent, hand near
body; on third hop, do big jump and bring R arm out to R side.

Walk A to R (R-L-R), swinging from side to side; suddenly stamp S on L ft,
diag fwd R; A again, walk fwd on half-toe (R-L-R). Repeat, starting L.
Do all kinds of lazy, relaxed steps using hips and sudden stops, as though
suddenly surprised.

Go backward: step back on L ft, R pointed front, body bent back all the time.
Each time you take a step, bounce back a little further.

Step L on L ft, bringing R arm over L; put R ft crossed over in back of L ft
(to L side); bend way over L; step L ft crossed over in back of R ft, bending
way back (circular movement of body); step R on R ft. Repeat to same side.

Walk backward, swaying from side to side, both arms out to side, shoulder-
high; while swaying, do fwd round movement of the pelvis; when weight
moves R to R ft, sway whole upper body and head over R, slightly fwd.
Stay all the time bending back, only move from side to side.

Step fwd on L ft; bring R ft up to L ft in 1st pos, feet together, jumping into
deep plié; straighten, wiggling hips and shoulders from side to side. Repeat,
doing figure eight with hips and finishing it in upper body. Repeat, facing
sideward and with side movement of hips.

CHICAGO, 1935

Go fwd (back to public): step back plié on R ft, at same time lifting arms
out to side and up overhead, bending back. Step back on L ft. Step back
plié on R ft, at same time bending fwd.

Go backward: step on half-toe, lifting other leg straight in front (not too high),
at same time lifting arms out to side and up overhead, bending way back;
bring lifted leg down. Repeat on same ft.

Go fwd: step on R half-toe, L leg up in arabesque; stretch R arm abruptly up S straight overhead; suddenly do same with L arm; bring L leg down in front, 4th pos plié, everything A.

Go fwd: rise on R half-toe; bend slightly back, at same time lifting L leg very straight in front (not high); lift shoulders, arms straight down at sides, hands touching sides of legs S; two steps fwd A. Repeat. (Take breath as you rise on half-toe and let it out as you walk fwd.) Go backward, kicking head each time (with swing).

Go diag fwd R, facing C8: step on L half-toe; bring R ft half-toe up to L; lean diag fwd as far as possible until you fall diag fwd on R ft in lunge; put L arm out L, stretching it as far away from body as possible.

Rise on L half-toe, lifting R leg very little, knee bent in front; come down on R ft in deep plié (big 4th pos); leaving lifted R shoulder up, circle R hand, turning hand in-out; end with R hand down to R side (like a sigh).

Do quick turns (déboulés) with arms straight out to side; end with arms in close to body, one in front and one in back. Repeat, all the time bending back (stay in backbend). Repeat, R arm out to R side, head lying on R shoulder; as you turn, keep stretching further and further out to R side. Repeat with big accent, jumping in 2nd pos on every eighth count.

Two steps fwd, plié in 4th pos, weight on front ft; swing R arm way around R, bending body down to R side, then twisting way to back. Repeat to other side.

2nd pos. Lift R shoulder, lifting R arm; bend it up overhead to L, plié on L ft; lift L shoulder, bringing L arm across front of body diag fwd R, plié on R ft. Shift body to face L front corner like lunge (do not change placement of feet); lift R shoulder, lifting R arm overhead and down in front of L knee, bending over front with plié on L ft; shift weight to R flat ft, L pointed in place, still facing L; bend way back, R arm overhead.

FLORENCE, ITALY, 1936

Walk backward in big backbend, first with just one arm overhead, then with both overhead.

2nd pos; bend fwd without bending knees; bend knees; on seven counts, bring body back up, letting arms fall back; lift body up. 2nd pos plié, ankles rolled in; bend back, letting arms and shoulders relax; straighten.

Side bends. Facing L side of studio, go fwd: hop on L ft, lifting R leg to 2nd pos R, at same time bending way over L, L arm straight down at side, R arm straight up; step on R ft, L ft pointed L; bend way over R, arms in 4th pos, L arm en haut.

Falling lesson. Go fwd, stepping onto R half-toe, L leg straight up in back, both arms straight out to side; balance; fall fwd onto floor. Repeat, going sideward and facing side. Repeat, going backward, putting one leg up in front; fall back, doing little steps backward. Repeat, balancing, lifting first one arm, then the other on three counts; slide through 4th pos, going diag fwd R on R ft; lift L leg in arabesque, stretch R arm fwd, L ft back as far as possible; fall fwd. Do this very slowly.

Turning lessons. Start with slow foundation movements, then develop them into turns. Do turns on half-toe, both arms in 2nd pos; keep turning and bring arms in to waist, one in front, one in back. Turn with both feet flat on floor, going very hard from one ft to the other. Go fwd: step on L ft, putting R ft over in front croisé, then in back croisé, using R arm in figure eight. Go fwd: step L-R-L-R in four counts, turning L and bending way side and back. Repeat, with big backbend in one count, doing big sweep with R arm (very flowing).

Big accent step backward and backbend, opening arms to side on count 1; straighten on counts 2, 3, and 4.

Ethnic
Dance

E T H N I C *or national dances cover the globe, but their contrasts from country to country sometimes make me believe that the human body is not universally the same. I was made especially conscious of this when I saw how Japanese dances (from Noh to Kabuki) were different from Chinese (so brilliantly shown in the Chinese Opera) or how the islands of Bali and Java, which are so close together geographically, have produced such different styles of movement. Burma, Siam, and Cambodia are also close together, but very far apart culturally. However, all Indonesian and Indo-Chinese dance stems from Mother India. Most of the dances of India, excepting the temple dance, Nautch, deal with stories from the* Ramayana. *It is these stories that are retold in various ways by the dances of Indonesia. I certainly did not go to the Orient to write a book, but I was so overwhelmed, as any artist would be, by the beauty and intricacies of these countries that I naturally wanted to study their dances.*

In Europe, the dances of each country also reflect the national character, even though the countries are closer together than in the Orient. I saw everything from the Schuhplattler, so emphatically Germanic, to my personally favorite national dances, the Spanish. I first saw the Granada gypsies dancing out their fire and passion on the hard earth of their primitive caves, but these dances have now become so polished and sophisticated when performed by solo artists and their troupes around the world that one tends to think of them as "classical" Spanish dance.

UNESCO's International Dance Council, of which I was a member, is doing everything possible to preserve all these dances, especially on film. These films, and many others from all over the world, are in the archives of the Dance Collection of the Performing Arts Research Center, The New York Public Library at Lincoln Center. Every dancer should try to see these films and to study in as many "character" classes as possible to learn what the human body can really express.

Mitsugoro Bando, 1928

FAR EASTERN DANCING
1928-1929

JAPAN *September 17–October 16, 1928*

In 1928, I was invited to give thirty concerts during the ceremonies enthroning the Emperor Hirohito in Tokyo. Of course, I accepted with alacrity. My experience in Japan was exciting from beginning to end: the audiences were extraordinary and the critics and press who interviewed me knew all my ballets and solo dances, where they were created, and when.

Wanting to learn as much as possible about Japanese dance, I was lucky to have as my teacher Mitsugoro Bando,[4] one of the greatest Japanese actor-dancers. Every morning I had a private lesson with Mitsugoro. I had to be careful about what I wore, because a charming female attendant always undressed me, folded my clothes, and put them away. I do not know how or if the Japanese teach straight technique the way we do in ballet; it seems to come from studying the dances. You have to be able to manage the big sleeves and the long kimonos, and fans (handled so subtly) seem to be an important prop in many of their dances. I learned a delicate, very refined solo in which I held a small tambourine in each hand. My kimono was black, with long white and black sleeves and train. The scene consisted of a gold screen on a hollow platform, so that all the little foot stamps could be heard. I called the dance Japanese Print, *and included it in my solo programs. It was the first and last time I ever tried to be authentic.*

The theatre in Japan—classical Noh, popular Kabuki, and doll theatre (many movements of which had been incorporated into Kabuki)—seemed to be flourishing at the time. These theatrical styles combined drama and dance so effectively because the actors were also fine dancers. Most of these actor-dancers performed their traditional roles in the Kabuki theatre, simultaneously training their sons to replace them as onagatas, *male artists famous for their portrayals of women.*

I saw a great many solos, each with a big underlying idea. I especially remember Kikugoro Onoye in one of the old Kabuki dances with words. In his slow movements, the dancer seemed to sink into the collective consciousness of his undemonstrative audience. By comparison, our solos, lasting between three and five minutes, seemed fleeting. The content of

---

[4]b. Tokyo, 1882–d. Tokyo, 1961.

117

Dodoji at the Dodoji Temple

the Japanese dances, repeated generation after generation with the same ideas and movements, totally absorbed the personality of the dancer.

I also saw many Noh performances. While it was not a popular form of theatre dance, I was fascinated by the intense rhythms of the strange voices, the slow, studied walk of the dancers, the dramatic expressions of the masks, and the clean precision of each gesture. The ancient Bugaku dances were performed exactly as they had come from China centuries before. Always performed by four men, they were slow, solemn dances done in long, heavy costumes with great, white sleeves.

This worship of the past, this clinging to old ideas, was the great strength and also the great weakness of the Japanese stage in 1928. But when I returned six years later, much of the original meaning and symbolism of certain gestures seemed to be completely lost. Modern dance had gained a toehold in the Eguchi school, where the Wigman method was taught. Japanese embracement of ballet seemed to be only a matter of time. One always heard that the Japanese were not original in their art, having taken everything from Chinese culture in the past, and from the West in the present and future. Nevertheless, I found the dances of Japan profoundly moving. It is a country and a culture that will always be something very special to me.

SHANGHAI, CHINA *October 20–December 3, 1928*
I was not in China very long, and spent most of my time performing my own dances. In Peking, a fabulously beautiful city, I met and saw the great actor-dancer, Mei Lan-Fang, perform. I was introduced to this extraordinary artist of the Chinese theatre at the home of Mrs. Calhoun, the wife of the American ambassador to China. Although I did not have the time to study with him, Mei was kind enough to give me several of his magnificent costumes in appreciation of my dances.

In contrast to the splendor of Peking, Shanghai was little more than a tourist city that bore the squalid signs of the heavily trodden crossroads where East meets West. It was, however, a bargain hunter's paradise for shopping. I did have the opportunity to attend a performance of what must have been an example of typical Chinese dance theatre. It was called "The Ten Golden Fans," and I wrote down my notes on it before leaving China for the exotic sights of Indochina and Indonesia.

Since that time, so long ago, I have seen the Peking Opera perform here in the United States, and I think it is as impressive in its spectacular acrobatic style as Mei Lan-Fang was in his profound solo works.

Mei Lan-Fang

CAMBODIA *December 6-11, 1928*

In 1928, I saw the whole Royal Cambodian Ballet dancing in the light of torches in front of the ruins of Angkor Wat. This temple is in the middle of the jungle, where the strange, piercing, and poignant cries of the tom-tom birds, the incantatorial chirping of the cicadas, and the tinkling of hundreds of bells added to the drama of the Princess, the Giant, and the Monkey King. Their stylized movements and the pleasant and serene expression of their faces flowed together in such harmony that I was completely carried away. The next day, I was climbing around the ruins when a huge snake wound itself around a bas relief of a dancer with her large, round bosom and very turned-out legs (such an exciting picture!). I stood transfixed for a moment, then fled with a scream. I always thought Angkor Wat was the most beautiful place in the whole world—until I saw Egypt.

At first, I did not write down any of the steps that I saw, because it was the whole that seemed important—the combination of song, words, dance, and pantomime. But I eventually learned some of the dances. The curator of the museum in Phnom Penh asked me to illustrate his lecture in Paris for the Gouvernement Général de l'Indochine; afterwards, the Governor General sent me roses. Although it was strange for a girl from Indianapolis to be so appreciated for her interpretation of Cambodian dance, it made me feel very important.

Angkor Wat, Apsaras on a mural

SIAM *December 12-18, 1928*

Siam seems so very far away—it is very far away. Somehow, I got there.
I was lucky enough to have with me a letter of introduction to Prince
Damrong, the uncle of the King of Siam. The Prince was very charming,
and gave a marvelous party for me at Varadis Palace on December 12,
1928. It was a night to remember. First, I gave a performance of my solo
dances, which seemed to fascinate the Siamese. Then, the whole Royal
Siamese Ballet danced for me—I was equally fascinated by them.

The dances told elaborate stories, mostly taken from the Indian epic,
the Ramayana. *The characters of the Princess, Giant, Monkey King,*
Demon, and animals (the latter two usually wearing masks) resemble

Royal Siamese dancers

those in other Indo-Chinese and Indonesian dance, but the style of presentation varies tremendously. The Siamese dancers (unlike Japan, almost all are women) use fourth and first positions and attitudes front and back (with plié) as in ballet; their hands, with fingers turned way back, are very important and beautiful and completely unlike ballet. Above all, it is the costumes that make Siamese dance most different. These are elaborate skirts and panels, heavily embroidered, with small wings from the shoulders or from the hips; slippers with toes turned up; and, especially, headdresses which, like Siamese architecture, reach heavenward in high, pointed peaks. The heavy costumes dictate the slow, solemn, and yet exciting movements. The dancers' faces are made up with very white powder, their eyebrows very black, and lips very red. Often, a white lotus flower hangs along the right side of their solemn faces.

At the end of the thrilling performance, where East and West really did meet, we were served a delicious meal prepared by the three daughters of Prince Damrong, Poon, Pi-Lai, and Chong-Chitr, who were learning to be "modern." One of them, wanting to please me, made ice-cream sodas, the last thing I expected to see in Bangkok, Siam. As a remembrance of this unforgettable evening, I was given one of the dancers' pointed headdresses, which I carried by hand in an aluminum box specially constructed to suit its proportions all the way back to the United States.

JAVA, INDONESIA *December 30, 1928–January 2, 1929*
I spent only a few days in Java in 1928–29, but I remember every second clearly, from the rijsttafel in Jogjakarta (served by twelve beautiful little boys, each bearing a different kind of food or spice to put on the basic rice) to the temple of Borobudur. This is not really a temple, but a Buddhist monument more than a thousand years old, with sculptured reliefs telling the story of Buddha's life from instruction and prophecies to serene contemplation. The dancing I saw in Java seemed to be an animation of these reliefs.

People say that Balinese art comes directly from Java. To me, Balinese and Javanese dances seemed very different indeed. In Java, I did not take any lessons, but I took notes on what I saw in a danced episode from the Ramayana. *It seemed almost religious in its slow dignity and even passion. If you could sit still long enough to absorb all the perfect control, you were rewarded. But I preferred Bali, a world of constant speed and vivacity, of darting here and there for no apparent reason.*

Javanese dancer

BALI, INDONESIA *January 3-16, 1929*
On my trip home "via ports" from Japan in 1929, I stopped off in Denpasar, Bali, to study their dances. At that time, American ladies were wearing very short skirts; the Balinese women wore skirts to the floor (sarongs) and no blouses at all. They were as shocked to see our bare legs as we were to see their bare bosoms. But Bali was really a magic island, both very primitive and very refined.

Bali's greatest dancer was Mario, who created a new dance called Kebyar. He squatted in the middle of the gamelan orchestra, which was placed in a square, and he never stood or straightened up. Under his

long-trained sarong, he held a cross-legged position, which is very difficult for a ballet dancer, and bounced up and down with effortless ease,
even when, every once in a while, he jumped into the air (knees always
bent) and landed in exactly the same crossed-legged position on the floor!
He flirted with the orchestra men, tapping them with his fan, and sometimes played on their instruments. His movements were sinuous, even
snakelike. His expressive face, with eyes rolling from side to side, sometimes frowned ferociously. At the same time, a slight smile trembled on
his tight lips, and his eyes would close for a second. No one who has ever
seen Mario will forget his genius. He was not really a teacher in the traditional sense. We did not speak. He did not explain. As a pupil, I just
had to watch his movements carefully and copy him.

The Legong, a dance for two very young girls (they reach retirement
age at puberty) was taught by an older dancer, who stood in back of
the child and pushed her arms and legs into the proper positions. It was
a religious dance to invoke the gods, and these two darting, dashing children, who clasped in each hand a gold-brocaded fan, must surely have

Teaching Legong

made an impression on the gods. They impressed the audience, which always seemed to be sitting under a spreading banyan tree, watching this theatre of trembling emotion.

There were also so-called "pleasure" dances, performed by the older girls, and stylized warrior dances, Baris, *for the men. Most special of all were the "trance" dances, in which girls stood on boys' shoulders, never losing their balance even with their eyes closed, until they finally fell down in a trance. There were others that added to the fascinating variety of Balinese dance, such as the witches* (rangda) *who fight with dragons in a struggle between good and evil. They all made such an enduring impression on me that I choreographed* Two Balinese Rhapsodies *when I returned home. I only hope Bali's dances have remained untouched by time.*

Two weeks seemed to fly by. I hated to leave my Balinese teachers and friends who had inspired me with their special spirit. When I told them I had to go back to America, one dancer asked me, "Where is America? Is it in Java?"

BURMA *January 29-31, 1929*
I wanted to see how everyone *danced* everywhere *in the Orient—a herculean task. My doctor father, who was travelling with me, wanted to see all* the hospitals *everywhere—also quite a project. So we agreed to do everything together. I must say, the hospitals of the Far East fascinated me, but I am not so sure that my father was equally intrigued by the often esoteric dancing to which I introduced him.*

I think the Burmese Pwe *really got my father down. It started at midnight and finished at dawn. It seemed that the favorite pastime of the Burmese people was reciting poetry ad infinitum, and Father, although he loved poetry, kept asking me all through the night if I had had enough. "No," I kept saying. "I'll never be in Burma again and I don't want to miss a trick."*

I had always been told that Burmese civilization was greatly influenced by China, but the Burmese dances seemed to me to be fast and lively, like the Balinese. The dancers imitated many movements from the puppet theatre, in which the puppets' legs and arms were manipulated by puppeteers pulling strings, sometimes producing a sharp, ludicrous effect. This was especially so when the movements were performed by live dancers.

The "puppet walk," as I called it, looked a little like some of our American jazz struts and used a pecking movement of the head, like a chicken. Giants, monkeys, and princesses were everywhere.

In the brief time I was there, which seemed like the twinkling of an eye, I tried to absorb and record all I could from my teacher in Burma, whose name I will never forget—Moung Mirama Senghejuon. Who could ever live up to such a glorious name?

INDIA *February 6–26, 1929*
I never actually had a teacher in India, but I watched all kinds of dancing everywhere. In 1929, I was in Delhi during Princes' Week and was more impressed with the pomp and display than with any of the dancing that I had seen. I did not go to the South of India, so I missed the great Kathakali story-plays and Bharata Natyam temple dancers. I did see a lot of Nautch, *which is a combination of song and dance, and supposedly imported from Persia. None of the* Nautch *dancing that I saw could compare with the theatricalized version created by Ruth St. Denis. Hers had more flair and was more spectacular than the real thing. Vera Mirova, a guest artist and teacher in Bolm's company while I was there, also*

Vera Mirova in *Nautch* costume, ca. 1920

specialized in Nautch *and snake dances. They, too, were infinitely more interesting than what I saw in India. Of what I did see, I was especially fascinated by the "cobra" dances, in which men pantomimed the snake with the use of a handkerchief.*

Pavlova discovered Uday Shankar in London in 1923 and engaged him to stage and dance with her in her ballet, Krishna and Radha. *I first saw Shankar in 1931, when he made a tour of the United States with his French partner, Simke (who looked remarkably like a native of India). Shankar was a great dancer as well as a beautiful man. Lots of women fell in love with him, among them, my seventeen-year-old friend, "Baby" Clow. So inflamed was Baby by the magnetically sensuous Indian that she firmly intended to leave everything she had in order to follow him back to India. Sensibly, Uday did not succumb to the alluring young lady, but instead urged her father to keep Baby at home. Shankar did not have his school when I was in India. It opened in 1938 and was continued by his son, Ravi, a master of the sitar. I understand that the school is the real guardian of Indian dance art and music.*

Rabindranath Tagore, the famous poet, and Ananda Kentish Coomaraswamy did a great deal to increase my appreciation of Indian dance. Coomaraswamy had an American friend, Stella Block, to whom he taught many native dances. Adolph Bolm (who was a great friend of Coomaraswamy) and I attended many of the lecture-demonstrations they gave; they were both marvelous.

Although I have never met La Meri, the most energetic American exponent of all kinds of ethnic dance, I greatly admire the fact that she has devoted her career to them. She has interpreted these forms in her own dancing, taught them in her school, and written any number of articles and books, including an important study of Indian dance, Gesture Language of the Hindu Dance.

I would love to return to India to see what is happening now and to study the vast subject more deeply. I do remember the Caves of Ajanta, which contain the most poetic and refined erotica that I have ever seen. India—ever mysterious, ever enticing poets, musicians, and dancers to her vast unknown world.

Chinese Dances

PERFORMANCE: SHANGHAI, CHINA, 1928

THE TEN GOLDEN FANS: Notes on a Play at Shanghai Theatre

Notes on costume:

Brother's costume is black and white coat and black trousers; very bold design. Nice costumes for men: black, tan, and white (something like *Prince Igor*); knee-breech trousers, short tight coats.

Elder Brother holds magic mirror in his hand (round mirror on stick with fancy colored paper around it). He uses it on the Tiger, which he captures and ties with a cord.

Funny old fat man, coward, with very thick black eyebrows and big, big nose, which Elder Brother finally chops off.

Magic-Horseplay. Bride always comes in with handkerchief over face, then takes long pink chiffon cord from gown. Lots of chasing around in circles, running very fast. Always use whips, and whirl them about in all kinds of ways. Lots of concubines.

Girls' Sword Dance

Girls' sword dance: two swords; much pirouetting and posing and whirling swords around very fast.

Girls: many movements with hands and sitting quickly on floor and getting up quickly during chase. One girl runs fast all the time on knees. Lots of pantomime. Shaking fingers and stamping feet when mad.

Man shakes R hand very fast and then shakes head, almost like Charleston.

Girl dances with two long sticks, an electric flashlight on each end and everything else dark. Effective.

Fighting: throw themselves into air and land flat on whole body. All kinds of jumping up into the air.

Girls often put hand over eyes—bashfulness.

Effective scene of gods in heaven with halos turning in back (like [Nicholas] Roerich painting).

Masks painted on face; only noses are false.

Little pergola. Girl hangs herself: two pieces of pink silk hanging from top, tied once; then she puts head in and ties it under her chin.

Conflict between good and evil spirit—shadowplay.

NOTES

Run on floor on knees very fast.

Love-making: hand in hand, they sway back and forth from side to side, arms around each other; they caress each other's faces with hands very stiff.

Cry: put one hand to eyes, other to stomach.

Fold hands, fingers interlaced and open. Lots of running around in circles.

Everything stylized, no expression on face at all.

Fights conventional: hitting sticks together. Both kneel with back leg way up, both hold on to same stick; pose. Very effective. During fight, Princess holds Giant's hand and walks around with him while he fights. Giant and Princess go off, arms around each other's waists. Just before end of fight, throw swords or sticks back and forth to each other.

Monkey usually good, usually comes to save Princess. Monkey King has a stick made of mirrors which he twirls around.

Little Prince flies away on back of a garuda bird; he has an unstrung bow without arrow.

Child dancer as the garuda bird

Elbow very loose, then extended until double-jointed.

Put hands on hips, low down, hands turned up.

Ugly man, who is really good, wears mask; takes it off and looks beautiful.

Naked boys rolling hoops: some wear hats and carry fishing poles.

All shades of yellow robes for priests, draped around brown bodies. They carry large pocketbooks, like large, round water jugs.

DANCING AT ANGKOR, CAMBODIA, 1928

Four girls with flowers in each hand. Kneel and put them on ground; stay kneeling and use hands.

Pose: one girl kneels with feet up in air, her back to other girl; other girl puts her ft on kneeling girl's ft. Very interesting pose.

Plié in 1st pos, walk on half toe very fast with plié low, then high.

Use shoulders a great deal and use body almost like jazz.

Go around in lines with gliding steps; stand on one ft, plié and up; go around slowly (adagio) doing a quick movement with hands on each turn.

SIAMESE DANCE

(Because the elaborate costumes usually conceal the positions of the body, the dancers are drawn here without costume)

1. *Princess Walk*
   Step R fwd flat with ft turned out
   Plié (L back 4th pos, half-toe)
   Travel toward C1 (L profile to
      public)

   R arm (elbow very ex-
      tended) straight, near
      front of body, R palm
      facing C1
   L arm straight back, just
      out from body, L palm
      facing ceiling, thumb
      and forefinger
      touching

   Continue, alternating four steps

2. Plié, L flat facing C2
   R knee bent in turned-in back attitude,
      lower leg straight up, ankle bent,
      toes near upper ankle

3. En face, R flat, with very deep plié
   L knee bent, very turned out, L ft
      just a foot out from R ankle

   Arms straight out from
      shoulder, elbows
      sharply bent. R lower
      arm up, wrist bent back,
      palm facing ceiling; L
      lower arm down, wrist
      bent, fingers back

4. En face, kneel R, L knee bent, L half-toe on floor, front

R arm out from shoulder to R side, elbow bent, lower arm up. L arm straight to L side, wrist bent up, thumb and forefinger touching

5. Knees wide open sit on heels
Lean fwd

Arms straight, palms of both hands on floor

6. Knees together and flat back
Sit on heels (both feet half-toe)

Elbows on floor in front
Look up

4

5

6

1. Typical hand positions used in Siamese dancing

2. *Typical position*
   En face, L ft flat, R heel just above L ankle,
       bottom of ft facing floor

3. Step R, facing C4   Arms in high 1st pos,
   Bend R knee and leave L knee   elbows bent, wrists
       straight, L ft flat on floor in back   bent and touching with
                                                   palms out and fingers
                                                   up. Look back at public

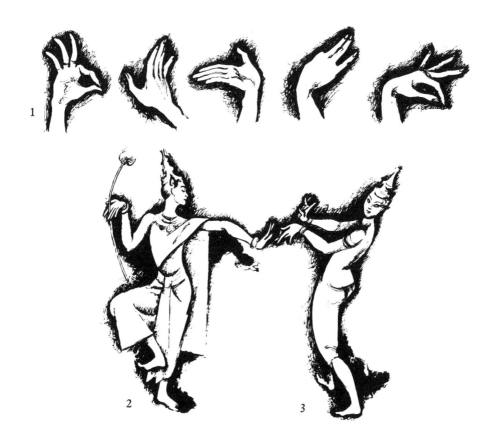

SIAMESE PRINCESS DANCE, BANGKOK, 1928

1. *Princess Walk.* Come in from back R corner. Step slightly croisé onto R ft flat, L pointed (half-toe) in back, small plié. Bring L arm through (very low) to front, inside of arm and palm facing front; bring R arm straight back, low, with back of arm facing front, back of hand facing ceiling. As you do plié, turn arms and hands just the opposite. (Lean head and bend slightly to L shoulder.) Step onto R ft and continue arms just the same, bringing hands through near hips, thumb and forefinger touching.

2. Start arms in front: L hand bent down, palm toward audience; R hand bent down with back of hand to audience, thumb and forefinger touching. Put weight onto R ft croisé; pose; L arm high and bent around, back of arm and palm facing face (only higher). R arm very straight and low, wrist bent and palm facing ceiling, thumb and forefinger touching. Step onto L and pose. Kneel on L knee, bring R knee to it, and go into sitting pos.

3. Kneel on both knees together and sit on heels, toes bent (half-toe) underneath. Put hands on thighs (above the knee), then lift them, leaving first finger till last. Turn hands out and bring them together (palms facing) just underneath chest. Pose and bounce on heels twice. Bring hands down and up again; bring them slightly up, then way down near floor (like révérence); bring them up to forehead, thumbs on forehead. Bounce twice. Bring hands straight down to below chest again, then straight down, but make a kind of little "rond de mains" with them before bringing them into place.

4. *Apsara pos.* Slide L knee fwd diag L, put R knee fairly close. Lift R leg up as far as possible with ft turned up. Turn hands open and out, then cross them and look up diag front L.

5. Get up on R ft; both arms turned with backs of arms toward body low down (very round), hands almost touching just below hips, backs of palms facing ceiling. Stand on R with big plié; L up in back, bent at knee, heel touching hip. Bring arms up overhead, elbows slightly bent and hands turned with palms facing ceiling.

6. Put L ft down in back croisé, and pose à la Siamois [see illustration 3].

7. Start Princess Walk (Step 1). Step on L, put R half-toe in back of L heel (like accent). Put R fwd and step on it. Continue this walk all around stage, moving arms very slowly and rather freely. Start with hands as in Step 2 (near L chest), bring them up and around slowly, gradually changing position of hands so that R wrist is bent down with palm facing audience, L hand is bent down with back of hand facing audience and thumb and forefinger touching (to R side) just opposite. Continue with arms until you stop walk.

8. *Moving offstage.* With back toward C3, put R ft way over in back of L (as though leaving stage); R arm also way over diag, elbow near body, thumb and forefinger touching; L arm stretched way to back, thumb and forefinger touching. Look back with eyes. Turn and do same to L. Exit with back to audience, both arms way back.

DANCING AT PRINCE DAMRONG'S PARTY

Festival in Heaven

Four boys and four girls in two straight lines. All very slow and long. When boys go up to girls, they take the girls' hands and the girls push them away.

Girls use quick movement of foot pushing skirts away.

Pas de deux

Woman, supposed to be a man demon, has a "diamond finger" which destroys everyone at whom he points. A god enters in the guise of a beautiful girl and the demon makes love to her. He caresses her face and tries to put his arm around her. They stop in the middle, every now and then, and talk. Finally, she says she will love him if he can dance as well as she can. She gives him a lesson and he tries to copy everything she does—it is quite amusing. She points her finger at herself; he does same, and is thus destroyed.

[*Monkey King and Princess*]

Monkey King does a marvelous dance alone, with cartwheels, splits, and extraordinary wide 2nd pos, lifting heels up and down. Sitting down naturally, with legs out in front, and running R hand up and down on floor (very effective). All kinds of scratching, and every pose imaginable.

Demon comes in, also hermit. Demon dances first, then Monkey King. They all do a pas de trois—very amusing. Monkey hangs on all the time to the hermit and plays all kinds of tricks on the Demon—very humorous. He jumps between his legs and scratches Demon's legs and face, etc.

Princess comes in. Monkey King has a love scene with her on the throne. She repulses him and he falls off a couple of times. All his movements are very quick and copied from live monkeys. Finally, he goes off with the Princess.

Girls carried off by garuda birds: girl sits in 2nd pos across man's back or on his shoulder.

Marvelous pictures of a blue god lying on a throne with two girls kneeling beside him. The throne is going down a lake shaped like a dragon.

Parasols over throne: nine circles for king and seven, six, five for lesser people. Effective as stage decoration.

Servant comes in on knees and stays on knees whole time, walking around from side to side.

Princess Walk, opposite arm and ft. Kick pleats in skirt.

Monkey King: cartwheels, scratch, shake head to R and L. Kneel on one knee, other leg stretched way out in back. Get up from that position, hands together on floor. Sit down naturally, both feet together in front, toes up, and scratch ankle. Wave hands back and forth and hop along. Jump from side to side. 1st pos, lift one ft, then the other. 2nd pos, plié suddenly with a jerk. 2nd pos, heels on floor, go fwd, wiggling feet. Walk along, putting heel down first as accent; move elbow and R arm with ft, other arm just moving hand. Pirouette (half) suddenly with ft up. Run, sliding feet—do not move head, only feet and arms. 2nd pos, sway from side to side.

Flower pos: wiggle thumb and forefinger.

Monkey and Princess: when he takes her hand, she almost slaps same hand while pushing it away.

In fight, stop long time in fighting pose, then continue.

JAVANESE DANCE, 1928–29

Kneel on R knee with L leg straight out at side; make salutation at same time, raising toes of L ft from floor. Rest R hand on R leg and L on L knee; do head movement to L side around and end with little jerk. Get up and move from one ft to another, throwing scarf around with both hands. Hold scarf with fore- and middle fingers, fluttering it like butterfly. Then put scarf around shoulders. Walk fwd, heel first, slightly side to side.

Wiggle head from side to side, doing all kinds of movements with hand near head as though looking around and hiding face, hands crossed facing face, then away from face. Flutter fingers in front of face. Keep forefinger bent.

Javanese Walk. Go to R, holding skirt up above shoulder with L hand. Step on R ft, put L back in jeté pos, half-toe. Change and put entire weight on L, letting R ft go to front, jeté pos croisé half-toe. Little plié. Soft, quiet. 2nd pos, half-toe, balance and sway side to side.

Start sitting on floor cross-legged, hands folded naturally in front with thumbs up. Salutation. Prayer with thumbs under nose. Head R, looking down L; then look to R, bend head low and jerk it to R (still looking to R). Finish.

Javanese Court Dance

BALINESE DANCES, 1929

[*Notes on Style*]

Everything jerky. Hit knee with closed fan very hard, then Bali Walk. Shimmy. Exaggerated hips.

1. *Bali Walk.* Shuffle along, plié then straight. R hand makes wide circles with fan. L hand does circles like jazz.

2. Kneel, head down. Sit on floor. Circle R shoulder very fast, then L. Get up suddenly and stand absolutely still on L ft, R up in front. Kneel again and repeat.

3. Repeat Bali Walk and exaggerate turning of hands with each step.

4. Sit on floor and fan yourself with R hand or slightly turned up and wiggling fingers, L hand quietly on knee. Get up on knees and stretch from one side to the other.

5. Sit on floor or stand up. Hold fan in R hand and move it in circles very fast (rotary movement with wrist). Move L hand half as fast, wiggling fingers, first to R, palm facing R, then to L, palm facing L. Keep bouncing either sitting or standing. Look with eyes to R and then to L.

6. Stand. Plié on one ft; put heel of other ft down with toes up. Put toes down and wiggle as fast as possible. Keep fan (in R hand) and L hand wiggling too. Shift head and eyes.

7. Sit on floor. Lean to L; L arm diag up L (bent), R arm bent and twisted. Slightly lift chest like big breath (for one count); on count 2, turn head and eyes to L. Effective.

8. Walk, putting ft down definitely every time; change fan in L hand sharply with each step. Move hips from side to side during walk.

9. Three steps. Close fan, hold in hand and point it with arm straight. Turn fan very fast while walking; hit leg (above knee) with closed fan. Before hitting, open both arms wide. Repeat to R, then to L.

10. Stand on L ft and wiggle R ft (keep half-toe on floor); R arm perfectly straight, inside of arm turned up, hand turned up. Grab fan: four fingers at back, thumb straight across front and sticking out to side (fan straight up); R arm rather low diag fwd R; L arm up diag back L, bent in curve, top of arm in, back of palm to face. Wiggle fingers. Turn head and eyes to L, R hip out diag fwd R. Step on R going to R; then on L, still going to R. Stand on R ft and wiggle L ft facing diag front. Lift L arm absolutely straight with hand turned up, back of hand facing face; R arm up and bent. Turn eyes and head to R. Repeat, starting to L with L.

Walk, jerking fan and L hand. Lift R ft up in front, cross it over, and put it down very hard. Move arms and hands up high over to L, then to R. Repeat, starting with L ft. Do this four times, going straight front.

4th pos facing R, R ft in front. Stand on L and wiggle R on half-toe; R arm up at side, elbow bent, fan underneath. Lean way over to L (L arm straight), nearly touching floor without moving pos of feet. On half-toe, turn and face other side; repeat, with different pos of arms. Look at L hand, almost straight back of hand to face. Hand up straight and wiggle fingers; R arm bent.

Pick up colored silks that hang from each side in same way as in Java.

Solo dance of girl with two parasols, each held by another girl. Soloist goes up to each parasol and poses.

Roll hips around while doing shuffle from side to side; L arm very stiff, R arm bent with fan. Move L arm up and down from shoulder and also R arm, sort of like a shaking back and forth. Hop on R ft, then L; come down on R very hard. Stand still and roll shoulders around. Repeat to L side.

(*Music:* "Ponka-ponka, ponka, ponk")

4th pos (should be done kneeling), R in front. Plié, jiggling all the time. Twirl fan in R hand fast; move L hand slowly. [Pose B:] On count 4, stand up very straight with jerk; put L hand, palm up, near L breast and bring R (with fan) up at right angle near R breast. Repeat, with some pliés. Pose B for eight counts. Continue fan movement with R and do slow, graceful movement with L, all from side to side, following hands with eyes. Turn suddenly and face R side; take pose (with jerk); L hand near L breast and R with fan near R breast. Turn to front and do kind of sliding step going fwd swaying hips, L-R-L. Turn, face L side, and take pose B. Swing L around to front, 4th pos, and repeat whole thing to other side, doing everything just the opposite.

4th pos. Twirl fan in R hand in front very fast, L hand going slower. On count 4, make little upward movement very quick and short. Repeat. Wave fan a lot and do pose B. Shake head. Repeat whole thing, taking pose B facing to side, instead of front. Go fwd with shoulders circling, arms back of shoulders at right angles. Shuffle in 4th pos.

"Tired" Step. Both hands near chest at side. Shuffle to L, bend to L side with jerk, bending head also. Do same to R, bending to R.

Shuffle from side to side; one arm straight and one bent, both moving back and forth from shoulder. Hop from one ft to the other with jerk; L hand moves (palm up toward audience) from R to L, fan hand also moves with jerks; head moves from R to L, eyes looking up to R, then down.

Beginning Step. Start with pose B, head shaking. Lift R ft and put it down very hard diag fwd R; R arm diag fwd R low, elbow bent, fan on outside of arm. Lift arm straight from shoulder, then bent straight up with wrist bent;

circle shoulder. Lift L ft and put it down hard diag fwd L; L arm absolutely straight, low down diag fwd L, L hand up, L arm up shoulder high and way back, elbow bent; bring back of R hand to face shoulder; circle shoulders again. Take starting pose. Go way down and come up with four jerks.

4th pos facing R. Wiggle R ft; rise on both feet half-toe and go straight to R side, facing R (sort of fast shuffle). Lower, turn, and face L (without changing feet). Wiggle L ft; rise on half-toe and shuffle to L. Do stretching step from side to side slowly, then fast, then down.

Face directly to L side. 4th pos, standing on R (hip swung way out to R and upper part of body way to L). Wiggle L ft in front; R arm straight to R side, fan (outer edge) pointing straight to front (fan on front side of hand), R thumb slightly up; L arm up in front, elbow bent, palm facing straight to R side, wrist bent with hand going a little back. Change and step on L ft; wiggle R in 4th pos, hips to L and body way over to R; fan to R breast and L hand turned up with palm facing face.

Face L, first just jerking and doing shimmy with shoulders. Face straight front.

1. 4th pos standing on L (big plié), R half-toe croisé in back; body bent over to R, hips way to L; L arm up overhead, elbow slightly bent, palm facing audience diag up L; R elbow bent with fan touching R breast.

2. Step back on L, just in back of R, both feet flat. Bend way over to L, hips to R; L arm straight; R bent, fanning yourself with R.

3. Step on L, facing L side. Wiggle R ft; L arm up shoulder high and bent, palm facing R side.

4. Step on R, facing R, L wiggling. Bend way over to L, R bent. Repeat step 3. Big plié; rise; shuffle, wiggling hips, facing R side; R arm bent with fan; L straight. Stretch from side to side. Repeat shuffle with hip wiggling facing L side. Stretch again, up high, shuffle.

LEGONG: BALI, 1929

(For two pre-adolescent girls)

1. Start standing straight (relaxed), feet about two feet apart, absolutely straight fwd (like primitive pictures), arms relaxed at sides. Wait like this all through introduction.

Preparation. Lift R ft up (bent croisé) in back, then L in front. Put L down hard (flat) diag front L; L hand at chest with elbow bent; R elbow bent shoulder high, back of fist to face, fan on outside of arm (pose A). 4th pos, L ft front, do deep plié, wiggling L fingers and trembling fan. L hip fwd, turn head and eyes to R. Rise. Plié again; start to bounce, at same time moving arms in jerk; get stronger all the time. End with shimmy;

Poses in the Legong

straighten both knees; lift arms and R ft. Put R ft down hard, 4th pos facing diag front R; L arm bent up high, L palm facing directly up; R arm low diag front R, elbow bent, hand twisted so that fan is up on outside of arm. Repeat, slow.

2. Shuffle step to R, letting body go before hips; R arm bent and twisted up high; L stroking side of body down then up. Move four counts to R, four counts to L.

3. *Balinese Walk.* Take pose A very definitely, lifting R ft and putting it down with a stamp. Walk around, lifting feet each time (holding body very straight and stiff). Go in circles or figure eights (different figures); hold L arm shoulder high, very straight and stiff, palm of hand facing front; hold R arm elbow bent, four fingers around fan, thumb up, and edge of fan pressed against chest (pose B, a very common pose). Walk four counts in pose B. Turn and change pose (pose C): L arm bent shoulder high, L palm facing up; R arm low, elbow bent, wrist twisted so that fan is up against outside of arm; bend knees very low. When turning during the walk, sometimes lift R ft up with a croisé swing (something like the Spanish) and set it down very definitely in pose B, before continuing walk.

4. Shuffle again (to side), this time letting hips lead. Turn body to L and sort of swing into the motion, arms in pose C. Move four counts to R, four counts to L. Do it with big swing and wiggle fan all the time.

5. Straighten legs; take pose A; repeat step 1.

6. Shuffle step, this time going very low on counts 3 and 4. Shift head from side to side, neck held stiff, all the time. L hand, when you go R, has palm facing R; when you go L, palm faces L; same with fan hand (R). When you go to L, look L; when you go to R, look R. Keep eyes moving from side to side.

7. Straighten knees; pose. Lift R ft up in back; put it down in 4th pos; arms in pose C. Eyes very steady, looking at some fixed point. Slow plié; turn head and eyes. Repeat.

[*Sequence of Steps*]

1. Slow plié, shimmy to both sides
2. Shuffle
3. Walk
4. Shuffle
5. Shimmy 4th pos
6. Repeat #1 to L
7. 4th pos, R pointed in back, plié and up
8. Shuffle (head shifting side to side)
9. Walk
10. Shuffle
11. Shimmy 4th pos
12. 4th pos (facing L side)
13. Walk
14. Stretch up
15. Shimmy 4th pos
16. Lazy stretch and shimmy, waving fan
17. Walk
18. Shuffle (facing back)
19. Small "hitch-kick" R-L, pose
20. Lift L ft and arm, slow turn
21. Slide L ft to L, then R ft to R, doing head shift

Note. When two dance *Legong,* they go to each other in middle of dance and put hands on each other's shoulders (facing each other), but one at one side and the other at the other side; they sort of pull each other back and forth. They also go to each other facing, kneel, and do the stretching movement.

8. *Stretch Step.* Start with L arm stretched out and up very high; R bent. Lean way over to the L as though tired. Start again like beginning of step 1. Bend fan hand (R) in very near waist; L arm straight up at L side; L hip way out to L side. Bring R arm very low (dip), then way up high and straight; at same time, bring L up caressing side. Move head from R over to L slowly (be sure to get head to other side before moving hip). Let R arm come down naturally. Repeat dip movement with L arm, R hip out. Keep doing from side to side. End with shimmy and fast twirling of fan in front. Take pose B and go into Balinese Walk.

Note. Stretch can be done slowly and softly or with jerks. Can also do same on floor.

9. Do shuffle step again.

10. *Slinky, slow step.* Straight knees pose. Slide L ft along floor and up and straighten it, at same time doing slow movement with L hand, palm toward back, then to front. Pose. Put weight onto R ft; bring arms close together near face, open them wide, and close again, shifting weight from L to R (ft to ft); use eyes.

End. Shuffle with back to audience. Still with back to audience, do hitch step, accent on L, to R, twirling fan and doing slow movement with R ft, four times R, four times L. Straighten knees. Stand on R ft; pose very definitely, with L heel diag fwd L; arms in pose B. Lift L ft rather high; put it down; turn to L, very low; L arm straight, palm facing direction you turn (L). Keep twirling fan. Face front; pose with R heel diag fwd R. Two glissades L with straight knees. Pose B with arms, only R hand has thumb down instead of up. Glissade R. End in big plié, pose B arms (thumb up); shift head and eyes from side to side.

MARIO B. 1897

Mario (I Ketut Mario) was born and trained in Tabanan, Bali. By the time Ruth Page met and studied with him in 1928, he was considered Bali's greatest contemporary dancer-choreographer and had recently created his most famous dance, *Kebyar*. Despite his legendary reputation in the Far East at the time, he was known only to those Westerners who travelled to Indonesia.

Nearly three decades later, Mario made a lengthy tour of Europe and the United States with the Dancers of Bali and Tabanan Palace Gamelan (created in 1880 by royal order). The touring company, formed at Mario's suggestion, consisted of fifty dancers and musicians, headed by Mario himself and I Gusti Ngurah Raka, his first and greatest pupil. The company came to the United States first in 1957 and again in 1962.

Mario was hailed as "the greatest living stage personality of the Orient," and, although well into his sixties by then, he was still dancing with "subtlety, dignity [and] nobility mixed with a touch of almost impish humor."

Mario, performing Kebyar, 1928

145

MARIO'S DANCE, BALI, 1929

Throughout, sit on floor with legs crossed underneath; bounce in time to music.

1. Pose 1: Frown, eyes wide open. R arm bent (in) below near waist, palm facing audience, two first fingers straight, other two bent. Look toward R hand; L arm bent at right angle, hand up. Circle both hands. Suddenly change to pose 2; eyes now look to L.

2. Pose 2: Frown, eyes wide open. L elbow bent in near waist, L wrist up and hand down, middle finger straight down and others up; R arm bent at elbow, straight from shoulder to elbow, then straight down, wrist bent with hand up, two middle fingers down.

3. Circle hands and go into pose 3: R arm straight from shoulder to elbow, then straight down, wrist bent with hand up; L arm straight from shoulder to elbow, then bent and continue straight front with hand straight up. Roll eyes quickly from side to side many times. Turn hands a couple of times.

4. Bring L hand to center, middle finger to center of chest and then out; bring R hand to center also, but away from chest and higher than L. Bring both arms out to pose 3, without stopping. Do twice, slowly and gracefully.

5. Bring both arms way over to R, low down; bring them up to diag fwd L (way up high), palm of L hand facing audience and back of R hand facing audience with fingers pointing toward L hand. Turn hands, R palm to audience and L immediately above it very close, L side of hand near ends of R fingers. Wiggle fingers (particularly of L). Move head from side to side, very small smiling expression, half-closed eyes. Go clear over to L; come halfway back and cross R hand (up to elbow) in front of L (near chest). Go suddenly into pose 3, then into pose 2. Lift both arms up diag fwd L; do hands like pose 5, going to R. Bounce up and down on hips. Start coming back to L. Come to middle; cross R arm way up high; bring L arm in front of chest, then higher; slowly put R down and pick up fan with fist (fan lies with handle to audience) and hold it down.

Fan Dance. Have L hand just over fan and wiggle fingers. Move L hand around and sort of in circles, gradually lifting both [hands]. Bring L arm and hand straight out to L side, elbow straight and wrist bent so that palm of hand is parallel to side of body. Stop. Move L hand slightly toward body. Turn it so that back of palm is parallel to side of body. Pose. Wiggle fingers. At same time, R arm is straight diag up R, fan on same line R, thumb pointing diag up R (same straight line).

Hop over to musician with both knees bent very low and put middle finger on his shoulder. Sit with legs crossed underneath. Drop if you can in that pos, L ft flat on floor.

Swing arms way around to L, L palm facing back L corner; turn and come back to center. Hold fan flat, outer edge directly facing body, L hand on top of it, palm facing ceiling. Come from down up with three jerks. Bring L hand (middle finger only touching body) across L shoulder and out to L side; bend elbow. R arm goes out absolutely straight, diag up R, fan exactly same line as arm; eyes look straight in front.

Do stretching movement (same as standing up). Go out to L side with L arm bent, then straighten it. You should almost lie on floor. Come up a little diag fwd R; lift up slightly before going down again. Circle with hips (must sit up slightly). Jump with both knees bent (as though sitting down).

MARIO'S PLEASURE DANCE (KEBYAR), BALI, 1929

1. Knees wide apart and sit on heels   Fan in R hand; hold skirt with L hand

2. En face   Arms out shoulder high: L lower arm up, palm facing public; R lower arm down, fist holding fan

3. Always sitting

> R elbow sharply bent, fan covering mouth; L elbow sharply bent, L hand near L side of face, palm facing public

4. R knee crossed over L, which is bent and flat on floor

> Arms 2nd pos, L wrist up, palm facing C6. Fan low at R side

5. Bend way over to L side

> L elbow bent on floor, lower arm up, wrist bent, palm facing ceiling

Head positions
Head goes R-L-R-L, eyes also R-L-R-L

Port de bras

1. L arm out to L side, L elbow bent and lower arm down, wrist bent, palm facing public; R elbow bent close to R side of body, lower arm out, palm facing public

2. Arms 2nd pos, wrists bent, hands up, palms facing opposite sides

3. Same as beginning with opposite arms

4. Arms out, L elbow bent and lower arm up, palm to public

5. Both elbows bent, L arm at L side, R hand on L wrist

6. Both elbows bent, hands touching at center chest, R high, L low

1. Sit on floor between knees, fan on floor open, outside edge facing you. Make big circling gesture with arms.

Pose 1. (Don't move) R elbow bent, hand parallel to R breast with fourth finger bending down; L elbow bent, L hand parallel to eyes (two fingers down). Look down to R. Make another circling gesture with the arms and end with same pose to other side.

2. Another circle of arms, ending with both arms out to side.

Pose 2. (Don't move) Both arms out to side, shoulder high and straight to elbow; R forearm goes straight down from elbow, back of hand parallel to ceiling; L forearm is parallel to ceiling, wrist bent, fingers point up to ceiling. From this pose, circle both wrists; movement goes to L and around. Do this twice, looking up to L as hands move to L.

3. Move L middle finger to body at waist (center) and up center of chest (touching all the time); bring R hand close to L (R follows L, but does not touch body); bring both arms back to pose 2. Repeat step 3, eyes going from side to side all the time.

4. Suddenly lean over to R, both hands close together near ground, way over to R. L wrist bends up and fingers point to ceiling (fingers wiggle from side to side all the time); R hand stays close to L wrist (natural pos) and trembles all the time. Balinese head movement [shift] continually. Gradually bring hands up to front L high, keeping head close to hands all the time. When arms get up there, change hands so palm of L hand faces R side wall; R hand underneath, wrist bent up with palm facing public. Go back to down R corner near floor.

5. Suddenly, put R arm over in front of L (R arm goes over to L, L over to R; R arm crosses on top). Go suddenly from this movement to pose 2. Repeat same wrist movement to L. Repeat step 3.

6. Suddenly and fiercely, another circling of arms.

Pose 3. (Trembling all the time) L arm low to L side, elbow bent. Lean over to L, L hand (palm) parallel to R side wall with fingers wiggling; R arm shoulder high, bent at elbow, forearm parallel to ceiling, wrist bent up. Tremble with R hand. Look intently down, then suddenly up (arms always in same pos). Circle hands to R (wrist movements), twice each time step is repeated, looking up to R. Repeat.

7. Bounce around a bit. Repeat step 6, taking pose 3.

8. Suddenly, put both hands way up high diag front L. Repeat second half of step 4. Lower R hand near floor.

9. Put R hand up (take slight breath to lift body) near face in front of body; lift L hand over R. Pick up fan with R hand, hold outer rim pointing to body (center); hold L hand, trembling, over fan, as though lifting fan by magic.

10. Do two jerky movements. End with R arm up diag front R, very stiff (inside of arm facing ceiling), wrist down, fist facing ceiling, holding outer rim of fan pointing up to ceiling; L arm up overhead (5th pos), two middle fingers pointing down. Do trembles with two L middle fingers up in middle of front of body; R hand still overhead, flat part of fan parallel to ceiling. Do two jerks, ending in same pose as beginning of the step.

11. Start to get up on half-toe, knees still touching floor; arms like 4th pos, L up. Hop four times to L in semi-kneeling pos (arms same). Put R knee on floor, L up; then L knee on floor, R up. Walk this way over to front L corner, changing arms in 4th pos from one side to the other.

12. Get up to slow music. Lean way over to L side; L arm down at side; R arm up a little above shoulder. Circle R hand slowly. Weight is on L ft with R half-toe pointed to R side. Wiggle R toes and L fingers. Come up and put weight on R ft, L half-toe on floor, diag front L. Wiggle L toes and L fingers. L arm is straight out diag front L with wrist turned up, back of hand to face (at arm's length); R arm is bent shoulder high, R hand near top of head. Look diag front L; do Balinese head movements to R; look to R.

13. Lift L ft up diag front R, put it down flat with a stamp; at same time, do same kind of movement with L hand, lifting it up and putting it to side emphatically.

14. Slow shuffle across front of stage, doing rotary movement with hips while holding everything else still; L arm straight out to side, shoulder high; R arm bent, fan near chest. This takes you to back R corner. Repeat all of step 14, ending in center not too far front.

15. Do this very fast: point with R half-toe, front-side-back (like dainty step); same with L ft. Do this four times, coming down to front.

16. Kneel sitting on both knees. Do movement like step 4 in *Religious dance* [Legong], only on floor instead of standing up. Lean way over to L, hand almost touching floor. Raise body and lean way over to R.

17. Rise all the way up on L knee and do movement something like step 5 of *Religious dance.* Turn hips way to R, look diag front L; both hands near center of chest. Sit down between knees and pose: L arm straight diag front L, back of hand facing face; R elbow bent, fan near back of head. Open eyes wide. Balinese head movement. Repeat.

18. Sit quietly. L wrist on L leg just above knee, hand turned up, fingers wiggle. With R hand, circle wrist near face as though fanning yourself. Lift body like a sigh. Repeat.

19. Put fan over face, leaving eyes uncovered. Go from side to side with head (Balinese movement), moving fan in opposite direction.

20. Quick music. Rise up on knees, wiggle hips from side to side; arms in 4th pos (L high, R low). Look diag up R. Sit down between knees; L arm up overhead; R straight up diag front R. Open eyes wide, look toward R hand. Repeat twice.

21. Roll body around front-side-back. Wave fan about madly overhead, circling wrists all the time.

22. Bow fwd, almost touching forehead to floor in front; both elbows bent, both hands near floor. Get up to sitting pos and pose; L arm straight to L side, shoulder high; R elbow bent, fan on R breast. Fast Balinese head movement from side to side. Stop with eyes wide open.

BURMESE DANCE

No. 1

1. L profile to public, facing C1
   Feet in "loose" 1st pos, deep plié

   Upper arms close to each side of body, elbows bent; lower arm out, waist high; palms facing floor. Look down

2. L flat (deep plié), R knee bent near L knee, lower leg in back off floor with toes up
   Lower body front, face public

   Eyes down. Arms shoulder high; R lower arm up, palm facing ceiling; L lower arm down, palm facing floor, wrist bent

3. Repeat first pose

   Clap upper thighs

4. 4th pos, R ft front, plié facing C2

> R arm low 2nd pos, palm
> facing ceiling, fingers
> up; L elbow bent, lower
> arm up, wrist bent,
> fingers down

5. Step fwd L flat, R half-toe
   Knees bent, touching each other

> Arms repeat

6. Kneel on L, R knee bent and out as
   far as possible to R

> Weight on L hand on floor
> (elbow straight); R arm
> straight along R leg to
> knee, R wrist turned up
> at knee, palm facing
> floor

No. 2

1. Weight R, L heel (toes up) to L side (about one foot from R), lean L. Body front, look to L

   Both elbows bent, one hand near each breast with wrists bent and palms facing public.

2.

   Lift arms overhead to 5th pos, palms facing ceiling (R arm lower than L)

3. Walk fwd with "pecking" movement of head (chin fwd then back repeatedly) in four steps, L-R-L-R

   Elbows bent, one hand near each breast

4. Weight L, R pointed to R side, body front, lean to R.

   Elbows sharply bent, arms shoulder high; R lower arm up, wrist bent, palm facing ceiling; L lower arm down, wrist bent, fingers touching L upper thigh

BURMESE DANCE, 1929

Burmese Walk. Step R-L, on full foot in place. Little jump onto R with strong accent. Do this all around room. Pos of arms on last count (weight on R ft), pose 1: L elbow bent, L hand near L shoulder; R out straight to side, slightly back. As you jump slightly, lift both arms up; on first two steps, change arms for pose 1.

(*A Good Ending.* Hit both hands just above knees (slightly plié). Jump onto R with L up in back, coupé pos. With hands still just above knees, shuffle straight fwd about ten steps (knees always bent). Sit down very suddenly: sort of jump into deep plié first, *then* sit down suddenly on L hip leaning to L on L hand, L knee bent; R leg further out to R, R hand over R knee.)

1. *"Jazz Head Step."* Come in and do step around in circle. Step on R with L heel on floor slightly diag fwd L; R elbow bent high up above shoulder, R hand just opposite R breast, palm facing in; L arm down, elbow bent at waist, hand up near L breast but lower than R, hand and palm facing away. Hold this pos. Stick neck (or rather chin) straight fwd; bring it quickly back. Step R-L-R (step on R, shift weight to L heel, back to R again), then do same with other ft, changing arms. Do this all around room.

2. *"Russian Slap Step."* Face straight front. Slap legs with both hands just above knees. Put L heel out slightly diag fwd L, and pose. Twist hands around and bend way over diag fwd R (down); R arm bent shoulder high, R hand near R breast, palm facing out; L arm straight, elbow bent up and out slightly and up high diag back L; look up to L hand. Bounce up and down a little. Slap again, go into same pose on other ft, but do little jazz plié in between while twisting hands. Do this step in place.

3. *"Pivot Step."* Slap near knees again. Pose, bending slightly to L (front); both arms overhead, palms facing ceiling, elbows bent R a good deal higher than L, wrists bent, fingers far back. Look to L. Weight on full R ft; keep R ft in place, pivot on it, and wiggle L ft. To make your turn, wiggle heel and toes and make complete turn. Look down at ft. Slap. Repeat to other side.

4. *"Pivot Step on Floor."* Kneel on R knee, R half-toe (R toe just slightly off floor); L ft flat on floor. Turn to R, wiggling L ft (same as in standing pos). Do one turn; repeat to other side, same pos, only put R hand solidly on R knee instead of up (for variety). Get up.

5. *"Jazz Walk."* Step on L; put R half-toe on floor in front. Step on R; put L half-toe in front. Regular jazz swing: hold skirt at waist with L hand (in front); R hand swings back and forth (front and back very low), elbow slightly bent up as arm goes back. Turn head L-R. Do this jazz step all around room. Kneel on L knee; L hand bent down, palm out (to audience); R hand bent up, palm to audience; both hands near chest. Get up, waving hands, and turn very fast to R. Plié suddenly. Sit down with jump on L knee, weight on L knee; L arm and R leg out (just like before) for ending.

To say goodbye, they just put R hand up near nose, straight up and down.

[*Burmese Movements*]

Jump like in Mario's Balinese dance with knees bent. Leap way up in air (2nd pos), cross feet, and sit down suddenly.

End sometimes in pose with back to audience.

Sort of jump into 2nd pos, land and lift ft in back jeté pos. Arms: one up, bent at elbow; one down, bent at elbow. Jump in 2nd pos again; land and other ft up in back jeté pos. Do very fast all around room.

Bend knees low. Lift one ft like in Charleston, only keep kneeling all the time.

Turn very fast with knees bent; sort of slide around; get up, continuing turn; down and pose.

Do movements like marionettes. Révérences. Come suddenly into funny poses with one leg up in back. Bow and scrape like marionettes. Collapse suddenly like marionettes. Also walk like them.

PERFORMANCE: NAUTCH, AGRA, INDIA, 1929

Pose, little finger on chin.

Thumbs crossed overhead, wiggle hands back and forth.

Kneel, sari overhead (skirt wide in each hand). Tremble scarf end from side to side. Accent with feet, still kneeling. Get up and turn. Movement with wrists together, fingers closed in. Three stamps to R; step on L.

Stand on one ft and pivot.

Skirt up in one hand only.

Heel tapping like Spanish, one hand on hip. Hands on hip like Spanish and rotate stomach.

Stand on one ft, other crossed over; wave arms around.

Scarf clear over face, except mouth. Cross all fingers. Hold scarf out over face, move it back and forth. Lift one eyebrow.

Hold skirt up in front and go around. Clap hands.

Notes on costume

Braid of hair: filled with flowers, big earring at end. Lots of flowers at back of head. Effective.

Skirt colorful: horizontal two-inch stripes alternating white, black, white, yellow; four-inch band of brick red at bottom, edged with gold braid; waistband orange. Very effective.

Scarf: edged with rough gold fringe.

SPANISH DANCING
1921 - 1929

Spanish dancing of all kinds has always fascinated me. It is usually learned by doing whole dances rather than isolated steps, although there are certainly basic taconeo *(heel taps) that one must learn for the* zapateado, *while playing castanets. I never learned to play the castanets very well because I never wanted to be a* real *Spanish dancer—it always seemed impossible to me not to detect someone who was not born Spanish—but just to use some of the material imaginatively for Spanish themes in opera ballets, for the four ballet versions of* Carmen *I did, for my ballet to* El Amor Brujo, *and for several of my "gypsy" concert solos.*

I am grateful to my teacher, Adolph Bolm, for sending me at an early age to study with Aurora Arriaza in New York. Maria Montero and her husband, José Alvarez, also taught in Bolm's schools in New York and Chicago, where I took classes from them. And, of course, I went to see all the Spanish dancers I could: Rosario and Antonio, La Argentina, La Argentinita, Vincente Escudero, the Cansinos. These were all great dancers with individual style and enormous audience appeal, but the Spanish dancers who truly inspired me most were the real gypsies who lived in the caves of Granada, Spain. They danced with bare feet, stamping on the hard earth (no floors at all), and were wild and full of fierce movements. These movements became refined when done by trained concert dancers. When I returned to Granada, everything was different: the caves had bathrooms and wooden floors. The gypsies had definitely become a tourist attraction.

From my earliest encounters with Spanish dancing, I have been impressed by the great variety of styles: classic, gypsy, jotas, country dances, dances with a long train, and more. Above all, I have loved the expression of the Spanish national temperament in every dance. Nothing is restrained as it is in classical ballet.

Maria Montero in costume for a regional dance of Spain

MARIA MONTERO
1890?-1928

Called one of America's foremost Spanish dancers, Maria Montero taught for Adolph Bolm in New York and Chicago. She was one of a multitude of Spanish dancers and teachers who flourished in the United States prior to World War II. Among these were the Cansino family (whose most famous member was Rita Hayworth), Aurora Arriaza, Juan de Beaucaire, Joaquin Ortega, and José Alvarez, who was Montero's husband.

Maria Montero was born in Spain shortly before the turn of the century. She claimed to have learned authentic Spanish dancing, not in the academies of the great maestros, but in the streets from the gypsies and in the cabarets. Due to family opposition to her career, she first danced professionally in London and throughout Europe before returning to Spain as a successful artist. Further engagements took her to Morocco and South America, and then to New York.

Her United States debut in June 1922 was at the Earl Carroll Theatre in *Pinwheel Revel,* a revue choreographed by Michio Ito. Aside from teaching, Montero concertized, specializing in flamenco, admittedly her favorite form of Spanish dancing.

"The keynote of all Spanish dancing," she said, "is dignity . . . I have seen artists in your country attempting to do Spanish dances, who seemed to have forgotten this entirely. They flip their skirts with the fingers at times, in a manner reminiscent of a chorus girl making a cute exit. It makes me want to cry," she lamented. "In Spain, a dancer never touches her skirts with her hands. She manipulates them cleverly with her knee and foot, retaining throughout . . . dignity of bearing and grace."[5]

She was eager to add, however, that "I find the American girl the quickest in the world to grasp the spirit of a dance as well as the authentic execution," and attributed shortcomings to managers and directors of musical shows and to unauthentic Spanish dance teachers.

A colorful and romantic artist of the dance, Maria Montero "died by a bullet from the hand of an importunate suitor on the evening of Wednesday, May 16, [1928]."[6]

---

[5] *The Dance Magazine,* November 1927, pp. 17, 58.
[6] *The Dance Magazine,* July 1928, p. 52.

CLASSWORK: MARIA MONTERO, CHICAGO, 1921

Spanish Steps	Port de Bras
(Waltz)	
Rond de jambe en dehors	
Pas de basque	
Balancé to R with R	Arm overhead
Balancé to L with L	
Repeat to other side	
Rond de jambe with R	
Step on R and rond de jambe with L doing half turn	
Step on L completing turn doing rond de jambe with R	
End with waltz pas de basque	
Repeat to other side	
Stand on L with L knee bent and R pointed out [à la seconde]	L arm up; R low
Close R ft front in 5th pos (twice)	
Three steps to R	Lifting L arm
Repeat to other side	
Stand on L and stamp (short one) with R in 5th pos	
Bigger stamp further away (relax body and on second stamp, stick stomach fwd (as though someone had hit you from behind)	L arm up; R clear in back at waistline (actually touching back)
Two steps (L-R)	
Repeat to other side	
(Twisting step)	
Kick R up in back (touching L knee)	L arm overhead
Face R side	
Five steps to R side, starting with R	Gradually bring L arm down; R arm overhead
Face L side	
Bring L ft up in front, touching R knee	
Repeat to other side	
Step on R ft	Start with R arm up
Touch L heel on floor	
Step on L ft	
Travel to R side	Gradually change arms
Repeat, feet going to L side	Arms low around waist: R in front; L way around in back

Spanish Steps	Port de Bras
	On first step on L, shrug R shoulder and head low looking to R (very cute)
Stand still on L ft Plié Point R out and in, moving gradually en tournant	Start with L arm high Gradually raise R arm up to L Leave both arms overhead with back to audience
After complete turn, step on R Do regular Spanish kick turn [assemblé soutenu with backbend] (Aurora [Arriaza]) Repeat to other side	
Two steps to R side Put R heel on floor, then toe Lift R with little kick, at same time turning body from R to L	Arms low
Go straight front Kick R ft (grand battement en avant), then bend it, hopping on L	L arm high overhead; R low
Repeat same step kicking L ft Repeat twice (R-L) Regular kick turn, lifting R ft and turning to L Repeat *To go back:* Hop on L ft, kicking R to side and bending it Repeat same step on R ft, kicking L Attitude renversé turn to L, R ft in attitude Repeat	R arm high
Stamp, facing R side, One stamp on R Two stamps on L One stamp on R Repeat stamps to other side Two pas de basque fwd (R-L) Spanish kick turn R	Arms low around waist: R in back; looking to L

Spanish Steps	**Port de Bras**
Step on L	
High balonné with R	
Step on R, bringing L pointed into 5th pos and quickly out	
Spanish kick turn to R, lifting L	
Repeat to other side	
Pas de basque to L	
Hop on L, kicking R to side and bending it	
Repeat twice, changing feet each time	
Attitude renversé with R to L	
Stamp on R after turn	
Spanish kick turn to R, lifting L	
Pas de basque to L side	Arms overhead
Repeat to R side	Bring arms down gradually across body
(Jota Steps)	
Kneel: L knee turned in behind R heel on ground; R bent	R arm up
Jump and kneel to other side	
Pas de bourrée	
Jeté en tournant to R	
Repeat	
Jota kneel to one side, then other	
Jump jeté en tournant. Very effective.	
Large, sweeping pas de basque en tournant in big circle	Swing arms, bending low

Jota turns from 2nd pos
    (jump like ballet) quickly to
    one side, then the other	

Step, kick front and into passé,
    doing "rond de jambe"
    close to knee. Effective.	

AURORA ARRIAZA 1868-1947

One of the most colorful, well-loved and influential teachers of Spanish dancing in the first third of this century, Aurora Arriaza had an extraordinary life from which she could draw to inspire her many students.

Born in Chiclana, Spain, Aurora was the daughter of Maestro Domingo Arriaza, who was a pupil of the great Otero. As head of a dancing academy in Seville, Maestro Arriaza had the great Carmencita and La Belle Otero as pupils. The young Aurora was an avid student of her father; by the age of twelve, she was performing throughout Europe. While on tour in Russia in the 1880s, the teenage dancer met and married Count Leslie, a Russian nobleman, for whom she gave up her brilliant dancing career. She remained in Moscow, and bore a son in 1895. Her days as Countess Leslie were rich in experience, but her husband's dissipation became intolerable. Deciding to return to the stage, she left with her son for Europe.

In 1900, Aurora formed a dance troupe called Las Bellas de Sevilla, with which she performed in London, Europe, and South Africa. In 1905, Oscar Hammerstein brought Aurora to America where she performed in vaudeville at the Victoria Theatre in New York and even in some Biograph films in 1911. After several years, Aurora once again gave up performing, this time to teach. She opened her school in New York at 637 Madison Avenue, on December 2, 1918, and taught until ill health incapacitated her. After a long illness, she died in New York.

"I have continually met with the unnecessary claim of Spanish descent on the part of many of my pupils," Arriaza said, "who were suffering from the delusion that only the Spanish can make good Spanish dancers." This, she considered, was "far from the truth." In fact, she claimed to have found "as many great exponents of the Spanish style among artists of other national derivations as among the Spanish."

A list of her pupils supports this claim and includes (besides Ruth Page) Martha Graham, Helen Tamiris, Carola Goya, Chester Hale, Leon Leonidoff, Felicia Sorel, Doris Niles, Nita Naldi, and even Rudolph Valentino's wife, Natasha Rambova.

In a 1948 tribute, soon after Arriaza's death, Ruth Page described her recollection of the great teacher's method:

> Unlike most ballet teachers, she adopted the method of letting us *absorb* the dance almost unconsciously, then gradually sink into us without forcing—a matter of feeling entirely. Later I found out that teachers in the Orient also used this intuitive method.[7]

---

[7]"Salute to Aurora." *Dance Magazine,* November 1948, p. 18.

Aurora Arriaza, ca. 1911

CLASSWORK: AURORA ARRIAZA, NEW YORK, MAY 1926

Steps	Port de Bras
Heel, toe, and raise ft	
Three steps en tournant	
Repeat to other side	
R toe, heel, toe in 5th pos	
Kick R ft out to side, hopping	
at same time on L	
Pas de bourrée L	
Continue without heel-toe step:	
hop, pas de bourrée to L, making	
strong accent on first beat, bring	
R ft into 5th pos, kick out	
Criss-cross step going straight fwd	
(cross R ft in front of L)	L arm bent near waist
Repeat with other ft. (Effective to	
go fwd)	
Turn hopping in 2nd pos. Very effective.	One arm up
(*Jota*)	
Hop on R ft with L up in back,	
jeté pos	
Hop on L ft en tournant	
Hop in 2nd pos	
Hop, putting ft up croisé front	

Realito

REALITO (MANUEL REAL MONTOSA) 1885 - 1969

One of the great teachers of classic Spanish dancing, Realito was born and died in Spain. Among the many Spanish dancers who studied with him in Seville and achieved an outstanding international reputation were Antonio, Rosario, Estrelita Castro, Custodia Romero, and Carmen Sevilla.

CLASSWORK: REALITO, SEVILLE, 1929

[*A Dance of Seville*]
Man kneels and slaps floor. Claps hands and snaps fingers while dancing. Comes close to girl; holds out his R hand to her; lifts L up and down. Stamps as though pleading with her. He walks way back from her. Girl stands still, does "Oriental" movements with arms. Man comes up to her. Both raise arms overhead (5th pos), both facing same direction, and go around with heel-toe step. They barely touch each other with arms. She kneels, profile to audience and looking down smiling; he bends over her (effective if held).

[*Realito's Dance for Woman*]
Entrance. Come in from back L corner as though running away from some-one. Have cigarette in mouth. Stop, look back, shrug shoulders as though disgusted, then run back. Look again and walk back nonchalantly. Accent step: one step, weight on L ft; stamp on L ft; point R toe in and out very close; all en tournant. Move both arms up and across body, pantomiming movements, showing beautiful body.

1. Lift skirt with R hand (L overhead); lift R leg at same time; pas de bourrée with jerk. Repeat to other side, continuing in circle.
2. Run back to corner again, look for man. Come back, kneel on ground, both hands on head. Get up and throw cigarette down.
3. Weight on L ft. R ft in, then out twice. Two stamps with R ft. Pas de bourrée to L. Repeat to other side. Do this four times.
4. Weight on L ft, R pointed near L toe. Change weight to R ft, L pointed near R toe. Two steps; point L ft to L side. Repeat to R and L. End third time leg lifted up in front.
5. Go straight back, glissade; L arm overhead, twist L hand; move R shoulder.

José Otero, ca. 1930

JOSÉ OTERO B. 1862?

Otero, by many considered "the greatest living master of Spanish rhythms" well into the first third of the twentieth century, headed a virtual dynasty of Spanish dancing masters in Seville, Andalusia. His Academia di Baili at No. 67 Calle San Vicente was a mecca for dancers wishing to study the true and authentic Spanish dance. Second only to Maestro Otero himself was his nephew, Manuel Castillo Otero, who taught a class every night at ten to young ladies between the ages of seven and seventeen.

Otero's studio and teaching method were captured by one of his American pupils, Lisa Gardiner, in a 1929 article in *The Dance Magazine*.[8] The walls of the L-shaped room (about 20 ft x 8 ft in size) were papered with posters of bullfights and fiestas. Wooden benches lined three sides of the room, and a piano stood at one end. There was no dressing room, Miss Gardiner reported; a student danced in the clothes she wore to the studio that day.

The Maestro would sketch out a bit of a dance and then watch as the student imitated his movements. At the sight of a mistake, Otero became a "raging thunderstorm," but grew quite charming when pleased with a pupil's progress. His standards were always the highest: one must be a good dancer, or not dance. The range of Otero's temperament, his talk, and his gestures provided his pupils with the insight they needed into the passionate character of Spanish dancing.

When Otero completed instruction of the dance for the day, he would command his pupils, "Otra vez!" (again). After a rapid session with *palillos* (castanets) and *chinchiras* (finger cymbals), the master of Spanish dancing ended his lesson.

---

[8]Lisa Gardiner, "A Day With Otero." *The Dance Magazine*, August 1929, p. 43.

CLASSWORK: JOSÉ OTERO, SEVILLE, 1929

[*Terms*]
Media. Stamp once L, twice R
Entierro. Stamp once L, twice R, twice L
Secco. Stamp once L, twice R, once L

[*Stamping Exercises*]
Entierro, starting with L ft. Lift R heel, put it down; at same time, raise L leg to back, jeté pos. Raising R heel, kick L leg through to front; put R heel down. Put L leg down. Repeat, starting *entierro* with R ft.

Step-stamp R, step-stamp L, very fast one after another, bouncing up and down.

Entierro. Jump, turn to L. Two stamps in place; two stamps stepping fwd, opening arms.

Step on R ft, stamp L half-toe in front. Continue, alternating quickly.

Zambra (gypsy dance with tambourine)
[Hold tambourine always in R hand; use freely]
  1. Come in from back L corner, *entierro.* Three steps (slightly jumping) L-R-L. Moorish accent step: moving fwd, face L; stamp L ft, step R ft half-toe, in eight counts; on count 8, stamp L ft. Pas de bourrée (three steps

L-R-L) to L. Stamp R ft, three steps to R. Stamp L ft half-toe in back of R, facing front. Go backward (to L side, profile to audience) with kind of waltz step on half-toe for three counts. Down on heel; other ft (half-toe) in back—four times. *Entierro,* starting with L ft. Pirouette. Step on L ft, put R in back, turn to R (always jump with this turn).

2. Make little circle, three steps fwd L-R-L. Slide R ft through from back to front, accenting it with stamp and slight back-and-forth movement of body. During steps: one arm up overhead; on count 4 (accent step), arms come down, both to same side, with movement of wrist downward and close to body. Repeat to other side. On count 8, stamp with L ft and turn once on it to L, putting R ft around.

3. Straight fwd: *secco, entierro, secco.* Repeat Step 1 through waltz step backward. *Media* going to R. Repeat Step 2; finish circle with turn.

4. *Secco.* Step to L, facing R, both feet together. Repeat Step 2, each time lifting ft up in back jeté pos on count 4.

5. *Media* several times. Repeat Step 2.

6. Stamp on R ft (going to R side); L half-toe–heel; R half-toe–heel; L half-toe–heel. Start again. Do very fast to R four times.

7. Zapateades [heel taps].

8. Fall down to L, L knee bent, R knee on floor (leg from knee down and ft lying flat on floor). Get up very slowly, turn to L. Moorish accent step.

9. Little stamp like accent with R ft to R; big stamp with R ft to R. Two steps to R, L-R. Repeat to L (small and fast). During stamps: bring both hands up near body, bending wrists as hands go up.

10. Many *media* stamps going straight fwd. One pirouette to R; three to L. End standing on L ft, R pointed near L, both hands on hips.

Jota for boy and girl.   Back to back, touch tops of heads together. Each turns several times, without touching anyplace except heads. Effective.

PERFORMANCE: GYPSIES, GRANADA, 1929

1. Movement same as bull fighter when getting away from bull.

2. Two girls: one gets behind other, takes hold of her skirt, and whirls it around, following her in circle; back girl puts hand on shoulder of front girl.

3. Suddenly kneel on one knee; lift arms up and point them down, like banderillo.

4. Knees together, plié and roll them from side to side (like jazz).

5. Lean over; do come-hither motion with hand near face.

[Steps 6, 7, and 8 as seen in Seville]
6. Boy lifts ft up and down back jeté pos; accent step while leaning over girl.

7. Little girls kneel, hit castanets on floor; regular shimmy with shoulders.

8. Swagger walk; arm low, moving in opposition.

9. Step; kick; balonné front (small). Suddenly throw head back.

10. Bend knees and head low. Look sideways at audience; roll finger around near face at audience.

11. Roll hands all around hair, just above ears. Effective.

12. Put knees together as in Charleston.

13. Mandolin gesture: L hand near shoulder; R hand to body as though picking some instrument, jerky.

14. Go fwd, crossing one ft in front of other.

Gypsies dancing, Granada, Spain, 1929.
Photo by Ruth Page

POSTSCRIPT

Dancing is the most ephemeral of all the arts. It is up to the teachers to keep the rich traditions of the past alive and, at the same time, to proceed with new ideas into the future. Today, a well-rounded dancer needs to know ballet, modern, acrobatics, jazz, ethnic—just as we always did. But where can all this variety be found? Today's professional dancer tends to take a classical ballet class, of the most conventional type, every day. All the other stylistic possibilities of dance are learned on-the-job from choreographers. This seems to be the case no matter if the dancer is on the ballet, modern, or Broadway stage.

The difference between my days as a dancer and today is that all kinds of dancing, especially ballet and modern dance, used to be completely separate. As a dancer, you were either one kind or another. Those of us who wanted to be exposed to all styles of dance had to go from one teacher to another, teachers who were often the greatest living exponents of their particular dance style.

Now the styles are so mixed together that it is hard to say where one begins and the other ends. This mixture is the principal choreographic style of today (ballet and modern are sometimes indistinguishable). It all seems to have produced a blend with an overall sameness that often lacks the stamp of personality, the scent of spirituality, or the passion of a national ethos. That sameness is danced with a perfection of technique we never knew, but quite often it is artistically boring.

My advice to today's dance student is to shop around and find teachers who are sympathetic to you individually, who will give you what you need, not only in technique, but in the expressivity we found in dance styles around the world. I believe that dancers do not work alone enough —to know yourself is very important. When you know yourself, you will be ready for anything.

SELECTED BIBLIOGRAPHY: WORKS BY TEACHERS IN CLASS

TECHNICAL MANUALS

Albertieri, Luigi. *The Art of Terpsichore; an elementary, theoretical, physical, and practical treatise of dancing.* New York: G. Ricordi & Co., Inc., 1923. 140p.

Arriaza, Aurora. *Spanish Castanet Playing; unique and comprehensive method of self-instruction.* New York, 1924. 18p.

Camryn, Walter. *An Analytical Study of Character Movement for Dancers, Singers and Actors; an outlined course of study prepared for teachers and advanced students.* With illustrations by Robert Wolf. Chicago: Stone-Camryn School of Ballet, 1958. [Unpaged]

[Cecchetti, Enrico]
Beaumont, C.W. and Stanislas Idzikowski. *A Manual of the Theory and Practice of Classical Theatrical Dancing (Classical ballet) (Cecchetti Method).* London, 1922. 220p.

Beaumont, C.W. and Margaret Craske. *The Theory and Practice of Advanced Allegro in Classical Ballet (Cecchetti Method).* London, 1930. 97p.

Beaumont, C.W. *A Primer of Classical Ballet (Cecchetti Method) for Children.* London, 1937. 60p. Also a Second (1938) and Third (1941) Primer.

Wigman, Mary. *The Language of Dance.* Translated from the German by Walter Sorell. Middletown, Conn.: Wesleyan University Press, 1966. 118p.

OF RELATED INTEREST

La Meri. *Total Education in Ethnic Dance.* Foreword by Walter Terry. New York: Marcel Dekker, 1977. 127p.

Stuart, Muriel and Lincoln Kirstein. *The Classic Ballet: Basic Technique and Terminology.* New York: Alfred A. Knopf, 1952. 241p.